MENDOCINO

THE ULTIMATE WINE AND FOOD LOVER'S GUIDE

CHRONICLE BOOKS ❧ SAN FRANCISCO

MENDOCINO

THE ULTIMATE WINE AND FOOD LOVER'S GUIDE

BY HEIDI HAUGHY CUSICK

PHOTOGRAPHY BY RICHARD GILLETTE

Design by Sandra McHenry Design.

Map on page 22 originated by Chuck Dahmer, courtesy of Mendocino Winegrower's Association.

Library of Congress Cataloging-in-Publication Data:

Cusick, Heidi Haughy.

    Mendocino : The ultimate wine and food lover's guide / by Heidi Haughy Cusick : photography by Richard Gillette : foreword by Margaret Fox

       p.   cm.

    Includes index.

    ISBN 0-8118-1391-6 (pb)

    1. Wine and wine making—California—Mendocino County.

2. Farmers' markets—California—Mendocino County. I. Title.

TP557.C867 1997

641.2'2' 0979415—dc20   96-30618

                                     CIP

Printed in Hong Kong.

Distributed in Canada by
Raincoast Books
8680 Cambie Street
Vancouver, B.C. V6P 6M9

10 9 8 7 6 5 4 3 2 1

Chronicle Books
85 Second Street
San Francisco, California
94105

Web Site: www.chronbooks.com

ACKNOWLEDGMENTS

In appreciation for their inspiration, wisdom,

support, and counsel, we thank the following:

Barry, Brendan, and Shannon Cusick, Tom Liden, Glenn

McGourty, Norm Roby, John Schmitt, Rodney and

Charlotte Strong, Allen Cherry, Harley Hayes, Karen Silver,

Mendocino Coast Chamber of Commerce, Mendocino

County Museum, Mendocino Winegrowers

Alliance, Jasara and Holly Gillette, Zachary

Martin, Jason Wallach, Judi Connolly,

Ray Gorman, and Dan and

Bonnie Borghi.

HEIDI & RICHARD

CONTENTS

Foreword 10

Introduction 13

Overview
Map of Wineries and Food Purveyors 22
Wineries, Distilleries, and Food Purveyors
by Areas and Interests 23

The Wineries
Fetzer Vineyards 28
Frey Vineyards 32
Greenwood Ridge Vineyards 34
Handley Cellars 38
Husch Vineyards 40
Jepson Vineyards, Winery, and Distillery 42
McDowell Valley Vineyards 44
Navarro Vineyards 48
Obester Winery 52
Parducci Wine Cellars 54
Redwood Valley Cellars 56
Roederer Estate 58
Scharffenberger Cellars 62

Brandy Distillery
Germain-Robin Alambic, Inc. 66

The Breweries
Mendocino Brewing Company 72
Anderson Valley Brewing Company 74
North Coast Brewing Company 75

The Food Producers
The Apple Farm 78
Cafe Beaujolais Bakery and Brickery 82
Caito Fisheries/Noyo Harbor 86
Eagle Rock Gourmet Lamb 88
Gowan's Oak Tree Fruit Stand 90
McFadden Farm 94
Mendocino Specialty Retailers and Food Producers 96
Round Man's Smoke House 98
Thanksgiving Coffee Company 100
Alex R. Thomas & Company 102

Resources
Mendocino County Grapes and Wines 108
For Education 111
For History 111
For Grape Growing and Ranching 111
For Touring 111
For Wine and Food Events 111
Books 111
Magazines/Newspapers 112
Certified Farmers' Markets 112
Events 113
A Directory of Mendocino County Wineries 114
A Directory of Mendocino County
Food and Beverage Resources 116

Index 118

FOREWORD

The magic of Mendocino County is reflected in its transformations—grapes into wine, ingredients into dishes, an individual's dream into hard-earned reality. When I think of Mendocino's early and recent pioneers, I appreciate their enterprising spirits. I, too, have experienced how the heart's investment in a meaningful project in a beautiful place helps to reach one's goals. Without a doubt there is a romance to this area we call home. Mendocino's remoteness, rugged coastline, and stately redwoods lure travelers to its pristine, almost mystical endowments. Sometimes it only takes a glimpse for many to determine they too must become part of this wide-open landscape. Is it my imagination or does the vastness of the sea convey a feeling of limitless opportunity? However seduced by the obvious natural attractions, those who succeed here are in touch with more than their infatuation. A partnership born of respect for what the earth offers and a desire to participate in its cyclical, seasonal patterns also motivate those of us who are a part of this county's wine and food community. In this book, Heidi Cusick profiles a selection of Mendocino's food purveyors and wineries, and introduces some of the people who invest their lives making a living here. Richard Gillette's stunning photographs capture the area's beauty. The sights, tastes, and smells of Mendocino await. Those of us who produce these bounties are ready to share this magical offering of nature with you. Visit us in these pages. ❧

Margaret Fox, Cafe Beaujolais, Mendocino

INTRODUCTION

Mendocino is more than the beauty of the coast and the majesty of the redwoods, which together draw so many visitors. From the earliest days, the land and sea along this northern California county have been benevolent providers of sustenance. **T**he original population of Pomos and Coastal Yuroks feasted on mussels, abalone, crab, salmon, and rock fish as well as game, berries, greens, mushrooms, and acorns. When European settlers arrived in the mid-1800s with sheep and pigs; apples, pears, and other fruits; and vegetables and grains, they found a fertile and harmonious environment. Today, Mendocino satisfies many hungers, as a place to live or a region to visit. **T**he village of Mendocino has been my home for over two decades. Every day I pause to feast on the ocean view from my office window. Jagged rocks jutting into the sea are lapped by gentle white rollers one day, attacked by turbulent surf the next. From November through March we gather mussels from the shore, in December the crab pots go out under the bridge, in April we try our luck at abalone diving, and the rest of the time we acquire our seafood from other local sources. **S**everal times a month I traverse the sixty-eight miles from Mendocino through the Anderson Valley to Highway 101, our link with the rest of the world. A trip through this valley yields views of everchanging vineyards and apple orchards, each seasonally identified by its pruning, blossoming, ripening, and harvesting. December's lambs become meat by June or expectant parents by October. Gowan's Oak Tree and The Apple Farm have roadside produce stands filled with just-picked fruits and vegetables. Apple, pear, and grape juices are available at the Tin Man, easily identified just north of Boonville by its location in one of Mendocino's yurts, a dome-shaped hobbit-like building with red trim. **E**nroute on Highway 128, an eclectic assortment of wineries adds to the smorgasbord appeal. Seven of the twelve featured in this book are in Anderson Valley. Two other tiny ones with unique appeal are Pepperwood and Claudia Springs, reached by turning north on Holmes Ranch Road, about five miles from Philo. Another, Lazy Creek, with property adjacent to Roederer Estate, is a find among wineries and cultivates a devoted following for its Chardonnay, Gewurztraminer, and Pinot Noir. Hans and Theresa Kobler greet guests by appointment and share tastes and their European-style hospitality in a rustic setting at a picnic table. **A** little further down the road is Brutocao's tasting room, with its backlit, blue neon flying lion on the front of the redwood building. The winery is located in Sanel Valley on the east side of the county, but their award-winning Cabernet and Pinot Noir can be tasted here. **B**oonville, the biggest town on the route, is in the middle of Anderson Valley, which got its name from Walter Anderson, the first European to settle here in 1851. A few years later, residents of the valley developed their own language, known as *Boontling*. Although only one or two old-timers still speak the lingo, remnants are immortalized by signs on pay telephones that say *Bucky Walter* (named for the owner of the first telephone in the valley) and advertising for restaurants which says *bahl gorms*, "good food." You can pick up a book on the language at one of the shops in town. *Bahl gorms* are found at the Boonville Hotel and other restaurants with excellent Mexican fare, hamburgers, espresso drinks, ice cream, biscotti, and pub food. The Mendocino County Fair and Apple Show is held at the Fairgrounds in the middle of town every September. Sheep Dog Trials, worth seeing for the amazing canine skills demonstrated, are held at the Fair in July, when a huge lamb barbecue also takes place. More events are listed in the calendar section. ❧ **S**outheast of Boonville is a pastoral ride through the rolling hills of sheep country. Near Yorkville, vineyards appear. One, Martz Vineyard, up the hill, is known for more than its excellent wine. Goats play a big part on Larry and Linda Martz's ranch. In the spring, tiny kids are penned up in front of the tasting room to give children a

first-hand pet on these adorable babies. Goats are so important to the Martz's that their wine label features them. ❧ **W**hile Anderson Valley is home to over a dozen family-owned wineries as well as some of the best *méthode champenoise* sparkling wine houses in the United States, the east side of the county is where the biggest wineries are. Second only to timber in income, wine is the largest manufacturing industry in Mendocino. The first vineyards came following the Gold Rush in the 1850s, when European settlers planted grapes on the hillsides and ridges and fruits and vegetables on the fertile plains along the Russian and Navarro rivers. In 1879, Louis Finne is reputed to have established the first winery near what is now Hopland. By 1900, three thousand acres of wine grapes were being cultivated (today there are over seventeen thousand acres). As in the rest of the country, Prohibition put a halt to the wine business, at least for all public purposes. A tour of Parducci Cellars, the oldest continuously running winery in Mendocino County, is full of tidbits on the escapades and "growth" of vineyards during those fourteen years between 1919 and 1933. In fact, Parducci's labels tout the beginning of the winery as 1932. ❧ **I**n the beginning, Mendocino's wine industry was limited to local consumption, but as transportation of grapes and wine became more expedient, both were exported outside of the county. By the 1960s, Mendocino's wines were beginning to get recognition. Now the region is a coveted source of a wide variety of grapes, while wines from the three dozen wineries are taking a prominent place next to their Sonoma and Napa neighbors. The twelve wineries profiled in this book were chosen for their historical and scenic interest, extraordinary tours or wine programs, and easy access to visitors. They represent a sampling of

the stories and quality of Mendocino wine. The Redwood Valley Cellars Tasting Room, while having its own pioneer-family history, also features the wines of many small wineries in the county. Located north of Ukiah right next to Highway 101, it is a great introduction to the small producers, all of whom welcome visitors by appointment. ⁂ While timber brings in the most dollars, food and wine production play equally prominent economic roles in Mendocino, one of the areas in California where agricultural crops and farming are on the rise. In the last ten years the annual income from crops doubled to over $60 million. About twenty percent of the nearly seventeen thousand acres of vineyards are organic, and more are being certified every year. Half of the apple crop is organic. With huge wineries such as Fetzer Vineyards promoting organic grape growing and giving incentives to their growers to grow with no pesticides and herbicides, Mendocino County has become a national leader in the organic movement. ⁂ Geography and climate both contribute to Mendocino's allure. The altitude ranges from sea level along the western shoreline to six-thousand-foot peaks in the east. Serene valleys are wedged between the coastal and Mayacmas mountains. The Yokayo Valley, an expansive fertile plateau, is the site of Ukiah, the biggest town and county seat. The inland hot summer days and cool

nights make a long growing season of about 225 days a year, ideal for grapes, pears, and apples. The coast, with its even sixty-degree temperatures most of the year, is perfect for lettuce, peas, and wild mushrooms. Over fifteen thousand cattle and sixteen thousand sheep are raised in the county for breeding, wool, and meat. Dairy cows provide $2 million worth of milk, and sheep and lamb products account for nearly six hundred thousand dollars income. ⁂ The people who have settled this county, just a hundred miles north of San Francisco, have a long history of being independent vanguards and even rebels. In the late 1800s, the notorious Black Bart lurked in the chaparral-covered hills along stagecoach routes where he regularly held up travelers. Being so far from the mainstream,

opportunistic bootleggers found the protected Noyo Harbor perfect for shipping. In Anderson Valley, the locals developed *Boontling* so they could exclude outsiders from the conversation. Today, Mendocino County, known around the world as part of the Emerald Triangle, is home to marijuana farmers who vigilantly guard their illegal crops with the same intensity sheep farmers try to ward off the growing menace of coyotes and mountain lions. ❧ During the back-to-the-land movement of the mid- to late 1960s, Mendocino was a favorite destination. Hippies came to sell beads and eventually open shops. Artists, seduced by the natural beauty and dramatic coastline, are responsible for the dozen galleries in the town of Mendocino. Lured by a rural lifestyle and faced with the reality of making a living, an enterprising breed of creative people have opened cottage industries, most of which produce something edible. Or drinkable, as in the case of one of Mendocino's brandy distilleries, Germain-Robin, located in a remote corner of the county. ❧ Mendocino County is one of California's top suppliers of specialty foods. Wild edibles from both land and sea are harvested by resourceful entrepreneurs such as Eric Schramm, of Mendocino Mushroom, and Eleanor and John Lewellan, of Mendocino Sea Vegetables. With everything from cereals and condiments to beverages and desserts produced here, we can feast from breakfast through brandy on food made in Mendocino. Such delectables as raspberry vinegar, pear chutney, wildflower honey, varietal apple juices, blackberry jam, wild rice, sun-dried

tomatoes, air-dried nori, artesian mineral water, mail-order lamb, and whole bins of fresh organic vegetables are produced by people from Stanford graduates to former flower children. That is why half of this book is devoted to showcasing their achievements. ❧ **M**any of these products are found in shops and supermarkets both in Ukiah and on the Mendocino Coast, where tourism is a vital industry. Coastal bed and breakfast inns from Point Arena to Westport add to the romantic intimacy the area is known for. Three of the oldest hostelries are the grand family-owned Little River Inn, the elegantly Victorian Mendocino Hotel,

and the exquisitely situated Heritage House. Restaurants, cafes, and take-out eateries abound on the coast and feature the locally raised food and wine. Two daringly planted vineyards are within sight of the ocean. Mariah Vineyards, overlooking the village of Elk and Pacific Star Winery, right on the headlands near Westport, are scenic spots. ❧ **I**n addition to the food and wine, rich and varied theater, music, and art events are so abundant they feel as vital to coastal life as the pristine air is for breathing. Outdoor lovers hike along the headlands, in the redwood forests, and up paths in waterfall- and mushroom-filled state parks. Tourists and residents alike canoe in the rivers, kayak in the ocean, and bicycle the country roads. A ride on the Skunk Train out of Fort Bragg or Willits gives a glimpse of old-growth redwoods. A day on a sportfishing boat may bring in the catch of a lifetime. ❧ **W**hatever the craving, Mendocino satisfies. Crossing the county line on U.S. Highway 101, wait no longer to exhale. Traffic lightens. Gone are the urban stretches of straight asphalt and strings of franchises. In their place, the sight of food and drink at their sources promises a bounty like no other. I invite you to join me and have a taste. ❧

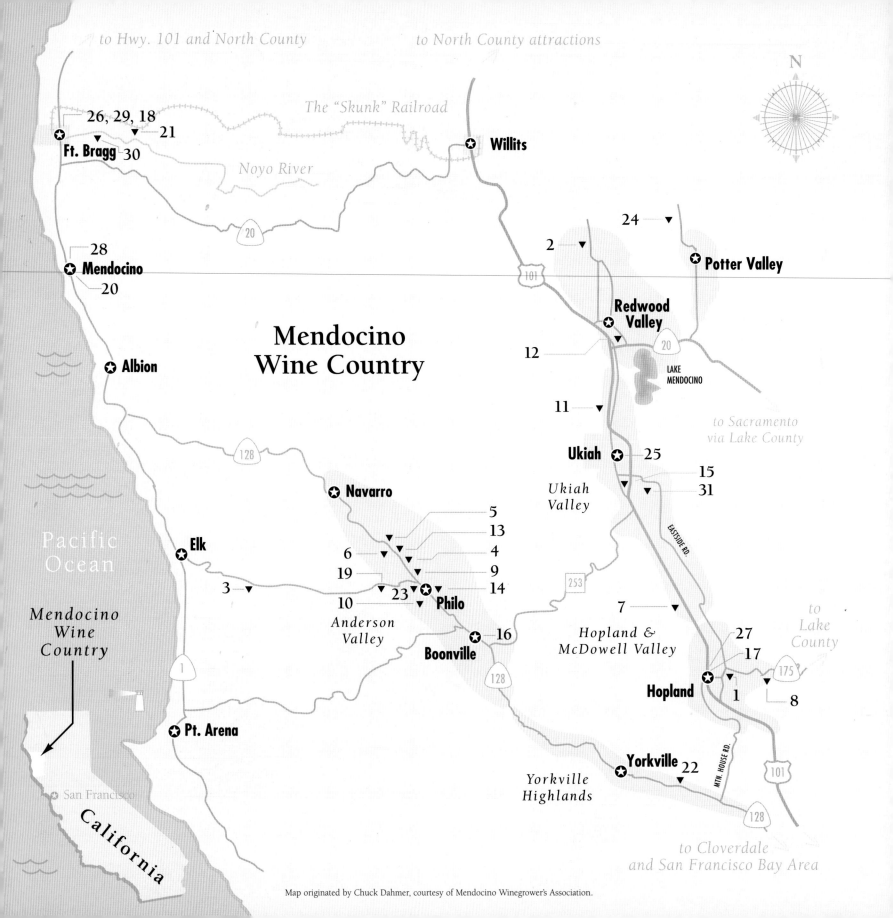

to Hwy. 101 and North County   to North County attractions

The "Skunk" Railroad

N

26, 29, 18

21

Ft. Bragg 30

Noyo River

Willits

24

2

28

Mendocino

20

Potter Valley

Redwood
Valley

12

Albion

Mendocino
Wine Country

LAKE
MENDOCINO

11

to Sacramento
via Lake County

Ukiah 25

Navarro

Ukiah
Valley

15

31

5

13

6   4

Pacific
Ocean

Elk

19   9

3

EASTSIDE RD.

253

10   23 14

Philo

7

Mendocino
Wine
Country

Anderson
Valley

Hopland &
McDowell Valley

27

to
Lake
County

17

16

1

Boonville

128

Hopland

175

1

8

Pt. Arena

MTN. HOUSE RD.

San Francisco

Yorkville 22

101

California

Yorkville
Highlands

128

to Cloverdale
and San Francisco Bay Area

Map originated by Chuck Dahmer, courtesy of Mendocino Winegrower's Association.

WINERIES, DISTILLERIES, AND FOOD PURVEYORS BY AREAS AND INTERESTS

MENDOCINO MAP LOCATER

THE WINERIES

1 Fetzer Vineyard
2 Frey Vineyards
3 Greenwood Ridge Vineyards
4 Greenwood Ridge Tasting Room
5 Handley Cellars
6 Husch Vineyards
7 Jepson Winery & Vineyards
8 McDowell Valley Vineyards
9 Navarro Vineyards
10 Obester Winery
11 Parducci Cellars
12 Redwood Valley Cellars
13 Roederer Estate
14 Scharffenberger Cellars

BRANDY DISTILLERY

15 Germain-Robin, Alambic, Inc.

THE BREWERIES

16 Anderson Valley Brewing Company
17 Mendocino Brewing Company
18 North Coast Brewing Company

THE FOOD PRODUCERS

19 The Apple Farm
20 Cafe Beaujolais Brickery
21 Caito Fisheries/Noyo Harbor
22 Eagle Rock Gourmet Lamb
23 Gowan's Oak Tree
24 McFadden Farm
25 Mendocino Bounty
26 Hot Pepper Jelley Company
27 Cheesecake Lady
28 Mendocino Jams and Preserves
29 Round Man Smoke House
30 Thanksgiving Coffee
31 Alex R. Thomas & Company

BY NEAREST TOWN

Hopland

Cheesecake Lady
Fetzer Vineyards
Jepson Vineyards
McDowell Valley Vineyards
Mendocino Brewing Company

Ukiah

Alex R. Thomas & Company
Frey Vineyards
Germain-Robin Alambic, Inc., Distillery
McFadden Farm
Mendocino Bounty
Parducci Cellars
Redwood Valley Vineyards

Boonville/Philo

Anderson Valley Brewing Company
The Apple Farm
Eagle Rock Gourmet Lamb
Gowan's Oak Tree
Greenwood Ridge Vineyards
Handley Cellars
Husch Vineyards
Navarro Vineyards
Obester Winery
Roederer Estate
Scharffenberger Cellars

Mendocino/Fort Bragg

Cafe Beaujolais Brickery
Hot Pepper Jelly Company
North Coast Brewing Company
Noyo Harbor Fisheries
Round Man Smoke House
Thanksgiving Coffee Company

WINERIES BY GEOGRAPHIC AND DESIGNATED VITICULTURAL AREA

Redwood Valley

Fetzer Vineyards (also in Sanel Valley)
Frey Vineyards
Redwood Valley Cellars

Ukiah Valley

Husch (also in Anderson Valley)
Parducci Wine Cellars

Sanel Valley

Jepson Vineyards
Fetzer Vineyards (also in Redwood Valley)

McDowell Valley

McDowell Valley Vineyards

Anderson Valley

Handley Cellars
Husch Vineyards (also in Ukiah Valley)
Greenwood Ridge Vineyards
Navarro Vineyards
Obester Winery
Roederer Estate
Scharffenberger Cellars

IDEAL VISITING SEASONS

Spring/April-June

Apple Farm
Eagle Rock Gourmet Lamb
Gowan's Oak Tree
Handley Cellars
McDowell Valley Vineyards
Obester Winery

Summer/July-September

Caito Fisheries/Noyo Harbor
Fetzer Vineyards
Greenwood Ridge Vineyards
Husch Vineyards
Parducci Wine Cellars
Alex R. Thomas & Company

Autumn/October-December

The Apple Farm
Cafe Beaujolais
Frey Vineyards
Gowan's Oak Tree
McFadden Farm
Navarro Vineyards
Jepson Vineyards
Scharffenberger Cellars

Winter/January-March

Germain-Robin Alambic, Inc., Distillery
Mendocino Bounty/Hot Pepper Jelly Company
Redwood Valley Cellars
Roederer Estate
Round Man Smoke House
Thanksgiving Coffee

WITH NOTABLE
OFFERINGS OF FOOD

Anderson Valley Brewing
  Company/Buckhorn Saloon
The Apple Farm
Eagle Rock Gourmet Lamb
Fetzer Vineyards
Gowan's Oak Tree
Hot Pepper Jelly Company
McFadden Farm
Mendocino Brewing Company,
  Hopland Brewpub
Mendocino Bounty
North Coast Brewing Company
Obester Winery
Parducci Cellars
Round Man Smoke House

WITH ART EXHIBITS

Handley Cellars
Parducci Wine Cellars
Roederer Estate
Scharffenberger Cellars

WITH HISTORICAL
OR OTHER EXHIBITS

Fetzer Vineyards
Gowan's Oak Tree
Greenwood Ridge Vineyards
Obester Winery

SPARKLING WINE

Handley Cellars
Jepson Vineyards
Roederer Estate
Scharffenberger Cellars

BEST PICNIC SETTINGS

Fetzer Vineyards
Gowan's Oak Tree
Greenwood Ridge Vineyards
Handley Cellars
Husch Vineyards
Obester Winery
Navarro Vineyards
Parducci Wine Cellars
Redwood Valley Cellars
Scharffenberger Cellars

OUTSTANDING TOURS

Anderson Valley Brewing
  Company
The Apple Farm
Fetzer Vineyards
Germain-Robin Alambic, Inc.,
  Distillery
McDowell Valley Vineyards
McFadden Farm
Mendocino Brewing Company
North Coast Brewing Company
Parducci Wine Cellars
Thanksgiving Coffee

SELF-GUIDED TOURS

Fetzer Vineyards (garden)
Husch Vineyards (vineyard)

WITH FOOD- AND
WINE-RELATED EVENTS

The Apple Farm
Fetzer Vineyards
Gowan's Oak Tree
Greenwood Ridge Vineyards
Handley Cellars
Jepson Winery & Vineyards
McDowell Valley Vineyards
Obester Winery
Redwood Valley Cellars
Scharffenberger Cellars

FETZER VINEYARDS

FETZER VINEYARDS
Tasting Room and Visitor Center
at Valley Oaks
13601 Eastside Road
P.O. Box 611
Hopland, CA 95449
(707) 744-1250, 744-1737
fax (707) 744-9020
Winemaker: Dennis Martin
Winery owner: Brown-Forman

ACCESS

Tasting Room and Visitors Center
at Valley Oaks
Location: From Highway 101, turn
east onto Highway 175 in downtown
Hopland for about ½ mile. The
entrance to the Visitor's Center is
straight ahead.
Hours open for visits and tastings:
9:00 A.M.–5:00 P.M. daily. Closed
Christmas Day and New Year's Day.
Guided and self-guided tours offered
throughout the day.
Appointment necessary for tour? No.
Wheelchairs accommodated? Yes.

TASTINGS

Charge for tasting? No.
Typical wines offered: Chardonnay,
Fumé Blanc, Gewürztraminer,
Johannisberg Riesling, Sauvignon
Blanc, Viognier; White Zinfandel;
Cabernet Sauvignon, Gamay
Beaujolais, Merlot, Pinot Noir,
Zinfandel.
Sales of wine-related items? Yes,
a whole emporium of wine and food-
stuffs here and in the Mendocino
tasting room, including logo glasses,
cheeses, fresh bread, and everything
for a picnic at Valley Oaks.

PICNICS AND PROGRAMS

Picnic area open to the public? Yes.
Special events or wine-related
programs? At both tasting rooms,
monthly events featuring wine and
food tastings. Hosts Mendocino Bounty

FETZER VINEYARDS IS CALIFORNIA'S PREMIER DESTINATION FOR wine, food, and organic farming. As Mendocino's largest winery and the sixth-largest premium winery in the United States, Fetzer is internationally known for its organic garden, food and wine education center, organic grape growing, heirloom seed saving, cooking school, and cooperage. It is one of California's largest composters.

I love it best as a place to spend the day. The meandering driveway under a towering canopy of elm trees makes an immediate transition from the rest of the world. Leaving the car at the far end of the property is perfect, for strolling is the only way to be indulged in the sustainable bounty I am about to witness. A short walk past the picnic tables under an arbor of climbing French Colombard grapevines takes me through the mottled shade to the door of the tasting room and country store. Attractive displays of cookbooks, condiments, local cheeses, and bread support the food and wine credo in a style Ralph Lauren (or Martha Stewart) would approve.

Tasting is fun because the variety of flavors and styles of well-priced wines are sure to satisfy every preference. On the young, white-grape side, the Gewürztraminer has a sweet and spicy flavor, and the Sundial Chardonnay tastes like ripe apples with some lemon thrown in. Fetzer's Barrel Select Sauvignon Blanc and Merlot are classic examples of their varietals. This is one of the few places in Mendocino County to taste Gamay Beaujolais and Johannisberg Riesling wines. Fetzer's slogan "from the earth to the table" is exemplified when it comes to their Bonterra Chardonnay or Cabernet Sauvignon, both made exclusively from organically-grown grapes. The outgoing staff readily shares details on the technicalities of wine production as well as on Fetzer's food and wine program. They also relate some of Fetzer's history.

Barney Fetzer was a lumber executive in 1958 when he bought his first ranch in Redwood Valley, north of Ukiah. He raised grapes for home winemakers until 1968 when he began producing wine commercially. Ten of his eleven children eventually became involved in the winery after his death in 1981. They developed it from a 200,000 case to a 2.2 million case winery by 1992, when Brown-Forman, a Louisville, Kentucky-based company purchased it. The family-owned Fetzer vineyards still grow grapes for wine.

Part of the expansion in the 1980s was the purchase of the Valley Oaks property in Hopland. The old homestead was once a prominent chicken ranch amidst the hop-growing acreage. Now it is a visitor center surrounded by fifty acres of organic vineyards. The focal point of the property is the organic five-acre fruit and vegetable garden. Guided and unguided tours are available. Even though many of the plant names and facts about the garden are posted, a guided tour is the best way to get the personal touch.

The path to the garden cuts through the lawn where ancient oaks stand like towering sentinels around the hundred-year-old restored ranch house. It's OK to carry a glass of Chardonnay along for some in-depth food and wine pairing right at the source. You may run into Fetzer's culinary director, John Ash, who is always delighted to share his suggestions for personal favorites.

After crossing the bridge to the garden, the first stop is at a landmark valley oak which presides over rows of tomatoes and garlic near the edible flower patch. It offers a canopy of shade on blazing summer days. Often a table is set up here with an array of tomatoes, garlic, herbs, flowers, or other just-picked produce to sample. This is a perfect vantage point from which to take in the incredible surrounding scene and to get a quick lesson on the biodynamics of organic gardening. All the beds are raised, which encourages root development, good drainage, and weed control. Composted grape seeds are the visible mulching material. Cover crops are companion-planted in between vegetables and herbs to attract certain bugs that would otherwise feed on the eggplants, peppers, squash, and corn.

Walking along the paths, I pinch a sprig of lemon thyme, a leaf of cilantro, or a day lily petal and note how their flavors go with the Chardonnay. Over a thousand varieties of fruits, vegetables, herbs, and flowers (not all of the flowers are edible) are grown in this garden.

Imagine being a cook with access to this abundance. One hundred kinds of tomatoes with names like Georgia Streak,

in August. Call winery for specific schedules and dates.

Fetzer Vineyards Mendocino Tasting Room
45070 Main Street
Mendocino, CA 95460
(707) 937-6190
Hours open for visits and tastings:
10:00 A.M.-5:00 P.M. daily. Closed Easter, Thanksgiving, Christmas Day, and New Year's Day, and possibly some winter weekdays.
Charge for Tasting? $4.00 applied to purchase.

Green Zebra, and Texas Wild, and dozens of types of garlic, overwhelmingly preface the possibilities. A dining pavilion and demonstration kitchen are located at the west end of the garden in the octagonal building next to Lake Fumé. Inspiration for the recipes prepared at Fetzer and shared in their colorful newsletter comes from the garden.

The garden is also what inspired Fetzer to devote its energy to organic vineyards. As the guide says, "We saw how well the vegetables and fruits did, but more important, we discovered how incredible they tasted. If the absence of herbicides and pesticides was responsible for this improvement, then why limit it to vegetables." Now all 360 acres of Fetzer's vineyards are organically grown. Another thousand acres of organic vineyards in Mendocino County are grown exclusively for Fetzer.

The organic approach to grape growing prompted Fetzer to look at other areas in which to increase sustainability. Its enormous composting program won it California's Waste Reduction Environmental Business of the Year award, and the new winery was built partially underground to save energy costs. Fetzer has also established its own cooperage to make and restore premium barrels from American oak. The generous sharing of the garden furthers the commitment to teaching what is learned here.

Summer offers the most impressive abundance of growing edibles, but a number of crops proliferate all year. Winter may find more broccoli and cauliflower than tomatoes and peppers, but there is always so much growing that visiting the garden is worth the trip in any season. My favorite way to visit includes putting together a lunch from the selection in the tasting room and then either hanging out at a picnic table with friends or moseying around the garden. It's the best way to take Fetzer's from-the-earth-to-the-table slogan to its natural and organic conclusion—from the table to my mouth. After my meal, I return my empty wine glass, browse through the flavored oils and vinegars made at Fetzer, and purchase a package of heirloom seeds. It may be time to leave, but it's never long before I'll be back.

FREY VINEYARDS

FREY VINEYARDS

14000 Tomki Road
Redwood Valley, CA 95470
(800) 760-3739; (707) 485-5177
fax (707) 485-7875

Winemakers: Jonathan Frey and
Paul Frey

Winery owner: Frey Family

ACCESS

Location: From Highway 101, take the
West Road exit in Redwood Valley.
Turn right on West Road; head north
approximately 4 miles to a stop sign
at a fork; follow Tomki Road to the
left 1.9 miles.

Hours open for visits and tastings:
By appointment.

Appointment necessary for tour? Yes.

Wheelchairs accommodated? No.

TASTINGS

Charge for tasting? No.

Typical wines offered: Chardonnay,
Gewürztraminer, Sauvignon Blanc;
Cabernet Sauvignon, Merlot, Pinot
Noir, Zinfandel; Late Harvest
Sauvignon Blanc.

Sales of wine-related items? No.

PICNICS AND PROGRAMS

Picnic area open to the public? By
appointment, weddings and events also.

Special events or wine-related programs? A Taste of Redwood Valley
in June.

A VISIT TO FREY VINEYARDS IS THE BEST WAY TO EXPERIENCE the definition of organic. In philosophy, according to Webster's New World Dictionary, organic means "having a complex but necessary interrelationship of parts." In agriculture, organic means not using herbicides and pesticides. In winemaking, the term gets a little fuzzy because of the debate on using sulfites. For purists like the Frey family, the word's meaning is perfectly clear—no sulfites or anything else that isn't a naturally occurring ingredient for wine.

Founded in 1980, Frey Vineyards is the oldest and largest all-organic winery in America. It also involves one of the largest groups of siblings in the business. On their beautiful acreage in Redwood Valley, near the headwaters of the Russian River, dwell nearly all of the eight sons and four daughters, with their spouses, and twenty-five grandchildren of Paul and Marguerite Frey.

Both doctors, the senior Freys bought ninety-nine acres to raise their children in 1961. Four years later they planted forty of the acres in vines, the most valuable crop they could think of, when pressure was mounting to build a reservoir to dam up Redwood Valley. Whether or not a property owner's liveli-hood had priority over a water source was a valid issue, the dam wasn't built. The vines didn't receive much attention until the 1970s, when the oldest son, Jonathan, after studying organic viticulture at college, took an interest. At first the grapes were sold to other wineries. Seeing the recognition the wines were getting under other labels, the family decided to bond its own winery. Now those awards are coming their way, and the Freys have become premier spokespeople for the benefits of organic wine production.

Call ahead for a visit. The last two miles of the trip are along Tomki Lane. Be on the lookout for the small sign at the begin-ning of the driveway. Then drive past the family house, a ram-bling redwood structure converted from an old barn. A small parking area is in front of the office, and to the right is the recently remodeled tasting room. In front of that is the original tasting room—a picnic table with a slab top and carved legs. Details like handmade furniture, carved wood decorations, metal etchings, and other artistic and eclectic touches are everywhere.

The tour is an organic immersion from the vineyard to the buildings and equipment made of recycled materials to the wine-making itself. Production is about twenty-five thousand cases; but with such a large labor pool, this is a very hands-on win-ery. Talking to any of the Freys, you realize they wouldn't want it any other way. A neighboring farmer said these are the nicest individuals he's ever known. No matter who leads your tour, you'll be introduced to other family members along the way.

The first stop, near the crush pad, is in the middle of a line of stainless steel tanks. At most wineries, these are the same nondescript containers lined up in military-like precision. Here each one is unique. Some list to one side; one has a design of a grape cluster welded on it; others are etched with whimsical or winemaking motifs. They are all recycled tanks. One was acquired after it was dropped when being unloaded at a big winery. Several were actually fabricated by one of the brothers. Another brother carved the shingles that decorate the offices and tasting room. Most of the building materials came from an old winery in Ukiah. Other things, like doors and windows, were acquired when buildings were torn down at the old State Hospital, where Dr. Frey worked until he retired.

In the cellar, cases of wine are stacked against one wall; a conveyor belt on another wall brings them in from the bottling line. When wines are bottled, matriarch Marguerite helps pack bottles in cases, although she still practices medicine in Ukiah. The logo on the label is from the signature of Dr. Frey, who passed away in 1991.

In the tasting room, Paul, Jr., another of the brothers and assistant winemaker to Jonathan, talks about organic winemaking. He hands out the winery's brochure, which explains Frey's commitment and what it means. As so many farmers are discovering, a big reason to grow fruit and vegetables organically is that the food just tastes better. It only follows that organic grapes processed as naturally as possible will make the best tasting wine. "Wine is the ultimate herbal extract," says Paul. "With the modern technology and equipment available that wasn't sixty years ago, we feel this is the right way to make wine." Previously, sulfites were necessary for stability and as a safeguard against oxygenation of the wine. At Frey, they go to great lengths to avoid air contact, which means carefully metering the amount of oxygen wine requires over a long period of time. Instead of cleaning equipment with sulfite rinses, everything is steam-cleaned and boiled.

White wines, which have a higher natural sulfite content, are more difficult to make organically than red. To compensate, they are kept very cold. All the wines have contact with oak and all go through malolactic fermentation, a naturally occurring process that lends a smoothness to the tannins in red wines and gives a buttery texture to whites. To demonstrate what can be done organically, the Freys make a complete line of red and white wines. Grapes for Sauvignon Blanc, Chardonnay, and Cabernet Sauvignon come from their vineyards. They purchase certified organic grapes for some of the above varietals and for their Gewürztraminer, Petite Sirah, Zinfandel, Syrah, Merlot, and Pinot Noir.

Frey wines are coming into their own as the family develops its winemaking style. They compete along with non-organic wines, and the awards are proof they are on the right track. When their 1993 Zinfandel won a gold medal at the World Wine Championships and received a score of 91 in the *Wine Enthusiast Buying Guide*, it was celebration time at the ranch. It's no wonder sales have risen five hundred percent in fifteen years. Now the Freys have set their sights "to quintuple sales again by the arrival of the organic millennium."

GREENWOOD RIDGE VINEYARDS

GREENWOOD RIDGE VINEYARDS

5501 Highway 128
Philo, CA 95466
(707) 895-2002
fax (707) 895-2001

Winemaker: Allan Green

Winery owner: Allan Green

ACCESS

Location: Tasting room is on Highway 128 in Anderson Valley, about 5 miles northwest of Philo, 37 miles northwest of Highway 101. The winery is on Greenwood Ridge-Philo Road on Highway 132.

Hours open for visits and tastings: 10:00 A.M.-6:00 P.M. daily, April-September; 10:00 A.M.-5:00 P.M. daily, October-March. Closed Thanksgiving, Christmas Day, New Year's Day.

Appointment necessary for tour? Yes.

Wheelchairs accommodated? Yes, at tasting room.

TASTINGS

Charge for tasting? No.

Typical wines offered: Chardonnay, Sauvignon Blanc, White Riesling; Merlot, Pinot Noir, Zinfandel.

Sales of wine-related items? Yes, including logo glasses, shirts, and Wine Notes and Brush Strokes Gift Packs.

PICNICS AND PROGRAMS

Picnic area open to the public? Yes.

Special events or wine-related programs? Anderson Valley Barrel Tasting in June; California Wine Tasting Championships, 4th weekend of July. Advance Tasting Club includes wine shipments, discounts, invitations to special winery events.

SO MANY INTERESTING THINGS GO ON AT GREENWOOD RIDGE Vineyards, it's hard to decide where to begin. Known as an innovator in the wine industry, owner-winemaker Allan Green is also an artist, designer, collector, disc jockey on the local public radio station, and music buff. The annual Wine Tasting Championships, hosted every summer at the winery, are his brainchild.

For all practical purposes, the easiest place to be introduced to Greenwood Ridge is at the octagonal-pyramid tasting room right in the middle of Anderson Valley. Driving through the gates, with their primary-color rectangles on heavy redwood, you might like to know that the unique architecture of the tasting room was designed by Allan's father, Aaron Green, who was once an associate of Frank Lloyd Wright. The building was built from the lumber of one redwood tree, which had fallen down on the winery property in the 1960s. After it was hauled out in 1986 and milled, not only the tasting room, but Allan's studio and office were also built from the tree, scraps of which are still being used for kindling.

The vines in front of the tasting room are samples of the varietals grown at the winery property on Greenwood Ridge, a few miles away. Classic-tasting varietals such as Chardonnay, Zinfandel, Pinot Noir, Merlot, and Cabernet Sauvignon, make Greenwood a good place to start honing your palate for the championships held in July. Contestants compete in the novice, amateur, or professional category, either as singles or doubles. Wine lovers with sharp palates try their best to identify varieties, appellations, and maybe even wineries. Just take a slurpy sip of Zinfandel or Pinot Noir, close your eyes, and commit those nuances to memory. Then have some fun and walk around the tasting room.

The untitled cork sculpture and Allan's collection of two hundred wine cans are worth checking out. The cans, which date from the 1930s, have names such as Vin-Tin-Age (California Port), Bigatti Vino, Canada Cooler, and Apple Splitz. Allan began collecting wine cans when his beer can collection numbered over five thousand and he had no more room to keep them.

In addition to the wine, the views of the surrounding vineyards, and the displays, Greenwood also offers one of the most unique gift packs available in a winery. Finding it increasingly mundane to describe wines in words, Allan commissioned two composers and three artists to taste his White Riesling, Sauvignon Blanc, and Cabernet Sauvignon and to create music and paintings based on them. The result is a gift pack, Wine Notes and Brush Strokes, which includes the three wines, a cassette of the music, and color reproductions of the nine paintings.

For the full tour of the ridge-top winery and vineyards, only six miles from the Pacific Ocean, an appointment must be made. While the music recommended to drink wine with at the tasting room is classical, Allan prefers rock and roll in the vineyards. (It's also the music on the radio show he hosts once a week.) As the tour guide, he tells you this on a walk through the vineyards, a spectacular event itself. Sixteen acres are planted with four acres each of White Riesling, Cabernet Sauvignon, Merlot, and Pinot Noir. At this twelve-hundred-foot elevation, with views spanning the redwood-covered coastal range, you feel like you are on top of the world. In the winter, the mountain caps are snow covered.

Allan's family bought this property in 1973, when he was still working full-time as a graphic designer in San Francisco. The beauty of the property quickly captivated him. He started taking classes at the viticulture program at the University of California at Davis, and began making wine as a hobby. By 1978, the original redwood winery, which has since been expanded, was built. The winery and shaded deck overlook the farm pond and water source. Stepping inside what was once the original winery, you are shown two underground rooms where barrels of Cabernet Sauvignon and Merlot are stored.

In the next room, barrels are stacked three high with a different variety in each aisle. Vineyard lots are kept in separate barrels until the final blending. A few stairs up and the door opens to the crush pad. This open-air structure is covered with a roof, a welcome addition during the heat of August and September. Visitors are welcome during crush, but a guided tour probably won't be available. Even without the tour, it's exciting to see the grapes arrive in half-ton bins and be dumped into the crusher. White grapes then go into the press, and the

juice is pumped into fermenting tanks. The red grapes go from the crusher into open-top tanks. Once used for milk, the polished seams of these containers make them easy to clean. Being quite shallow, they allow more surface area to volume, perfect for red wine fermentation. The shallowness makes it easier to punch down the cap of skins that rises to the surface, something that must be done several times a day.

From the crush pad, Allan leads the way to the warehouse for a tasting of current vintages. Most of the year, this part of the building is full of cases of wine awaiting distribution, but on the weekend of the Wine Tasting Championships it takes on a colorful transformation. Tables are set up and the contestants come to challenge their palates; afficionados come for the revelry. The atmosphere on this pastoral mountaintop changes to that of a country fair, complete with music and food. In recent years, chocolate and cheese-tasting contests have been added to the program.

Allan started the Wine Tasting Championships in 1982 because he wanted to get people to come up to the secluded site of the winery. Now that up to five hundred people participate each year and the tasting room annually courts 18,000 visitors in Anderson Valley, the Championships have taken on a prestigious life of their own with both amateur and professional wine tasters. They have become the benchmark of the innovative style of an otherwise low-key, mild-mannered winemaker. While the Wine Championships are incentive to taste a wine and learn to identify what you are drinking, they aren't the only reason to stop by. You never know what other interests and projects are being unveiled at Greenwood Ridge's Tasting Room.

HANDLEY CELLARS

HANDLEY CELLARS

3151 Highway 128
Philo, CA 95466
(800) 733-3151; (707) 895-3876
fax (707) 895-2603

Winemakers: Milla Handley and
Deny Dudzik

Winery owners: Milla Handley and
Rex McLellan

ACCESS

Location: From Highway 101, take
Highway 128 west 40 miles; winery is
on the north side of the road.

Hours open for visits and tastings:
11:00 A.M.-6:00 P.M. daily, May-
October; 11:00 A.M.-5:00 P.M. daily,
November-April. Closed Thanksgiving,
Christmas Day, New Year's Day
(some years).

Appointment necessary for tour? Yes.

Wheelchairs accommodated? Yes.

TASTINGS

Charge for tasting? No.

Typical wines offered: Brut, Blanc de
Blanc, Rosé sparkling wines;
Gewürztraminer, Sauvignon Blanc,
Chardonnay; Pinot Noir, Pinot
Meunier, late harvest Riesling.

Sales of wine-related items? Yes,
T-shirts, sweat shirts, hats, selected
cookbooks, and Mexican, African,
and other international folk art.

PICNICS AND PROGRAMS

Picnic area open to the public? Yes.

Special events or wine-related programs? First weekend of the month,
Culinary Adventure, pairing food and
wine. Summer, Expressions of Anderson
Valley, with music, food, local arts and
crafts. Groups can call ahead for guided
wine tasting and Culinary Adventure
for a nominal charge. CellarClub
membership includes wine shipments,
newsletter, pre-releases, discounts,
and special events.

CARVED ELEPHANT CHAIRS WITH TRUNKS RISING OVER THE wide teakwood seats elicit the first reaction of most visitors to the tasting room at Handley Cellars. Then come the English pub bar, African textiles, and tables full of colorful Mexican folk art. If you hadn't driven through a vineyard to get here, you might think you were in a fine art gallery, which actually you are. As you soon discover, the international selection of crafts isn't the only handcrafted specialty of the house.

Handley Cellars integrates art, food, and wine in a program known as Culinary Adventure that is shared with visitors at least once a month. With a menu of wines to complement every course, Handley takes inspiration from the surrounding folk art when selecting dishes to serve. If you arrive on a Friday, Saturday, or Sunday on the first weekend of the month, international delicacies are paired with selected wines. You might be offered sushi rice balls with the newly released Sauvignon Blanc, black beans in mole with Pinot Noir, or grilled jerked tenderloin with Blanc de Blanc sparkling wine. Music, too, is usually coordinated with the theme, be it African, Caribbean, or Latin American. Recipes are available to take along.

During the holiday season, and always around Valentine's Day, one of the prized sparkling rosés, bruts, or blancs de blanc is featured. Smoked salmon cheesecake is the annual favorite to try with Handley's sparklers, which are known for

tight bubbles and clear, soft hues, similar to their French champagne counterparts.

Starting with a taste of bubbly is a perfect way to tour the art in the tasting room, or to sit in the elephant chairs, gazing out the small-paned windows at the vineyards below. Better yet, wander out into the courtyard where picnic tables are interspersed among ancient stone carvings and porcelain statues. Overhead is a trellis of wisteria, an ethereal treat if you happen to be there when it's blooming in April. Throughout the summer, bushes of purple lavender perfume the air.

If you've made prior arrangements, you can take a tour of the cellar or the vineyards. I recommend the vineyard tour, including a stroll through the vegetable garden, which in summer is an edible jungle of flowers and vegetables.

As you go outside, you pass through the cellar. In front of stainless fermentation and holding tanks is an 875-gallon oval oak tank with a warm honey-colored patina. This cask is reserved for Handley's signature dry Gewürztraminer's short stint in oak. When wine is stored in such a large tank, less of it is affected by the wood, resulting in an intimation of oak in the flavor.

Through the winery doorway you pass the crush pad with its top-of-the-line Ames crusher and Wilmes press. The small vineyard in front is an experimental section with several varieties. Cover crops of beans, Austrian peas, and vetch are planted to fix the nitrogen and create organic matter in the soil. Different trellis systems are tried here to find out which do best with the light and weather of this particular location. On a split trellis, twice as many branches are left to grow as on a single trellis system.

Around the winery, thirteen acres of Pinot Noir grapes and nine of Chardonnay are raised for Handley's benchmark wines. The Chardonnay and Pinot Noir grapes for sparkling wines are picked first, when their sugar levels are around nineteen degrees, whereas the grapes for still wines are picked at a richer sugar level of around twenty-three degrees. The focus on quality rather than quantity informs all phases of winemaking here and accounts for the variation in production of between twelve and fifteen thousand cases a year.

On the other side of the experimental vineyards is the beautifully restored ranch house, which once presided over

the original acreage, a farm for cattle, sheep, and apples. Today the ranch house is used for entertaining and for housing winery staff and guests. To the left is the stately old barn, now storage for grape buckets and vineyard equipment: it was built in 1917, reputedly from the wood of one of the redwood trees on the property. To get to the garden, you walk around the barn. Grown to supply summer produce for employees and winery events, the garden is a continual source of typical and unusual edibles raised by tasting room manager Debra Deis, whose years working for a specialty seed company only increased her passion for gardening.

During the summer and fall, the monthly Culinary Adventures in the winery are determined by what is ripe in the garden. Corncakes with tomato salsa have been paired with Handley's fruit-rich Sauvignon Blanc, and a West African-inspired mixed peppers and carrot salad with the steely, food-loving Anderson Valley Chardonnay. The weekend pairings are samplings for the public, but wine groups and culinary afficionados also make appointments to partake in a more organized Culinary Adventure tasting. On Saturday mornings in the summer, you may run into a group being led through a tasting next to the ancient bronze temple lion in the courtyard. Handley also hosts an annual bazaar in the summer that not only features the winery's own food and wine pairings and folk art, but those of local craftspeople and cooks as well.

The adventure at Handley is thorough. It encompasses wine, food, and art while exploring untraditional pairings in a most educational way. Sidling up to the pub bar or plopping down on an elephant chair are the best ways to take this trip.

HUSCH VINEYARDS

HUSCH VINEYARDS

4400 Highway 128

Philo, CA 95466

(707) 895-3216

Business office: P.O. Box 189

Talmage, CA 95481

(707) 462-5370

Winemaker: Fritz Meier

Winery owner: H.A. Oswald Family

ACCESS

Location: From Highway 101, take Highway 128 west for about 38 miles. Winery is on southwest side of road, across from Roederer Estate.

Hours open for visits and tastings: 10:00 A.M.-6:00 P.M. daily, May-September; 10:00 A.M.-5:00 P.M. daily, October-April. Closed Thanksgiving and Christmas Day.

Appointment necessary for tour? Not for self-guided vineyard tour.

Wheelchairs accommodated? Yes.

TASTINGS

Charge for tasting? No.

Typical wines offered: Chardonnay, Chenin Blanc, Gewürztraminer; Cabernet Sauvignon, Pinot Noir.

Sales of wine-related items? Yes, including logo glasses, wine gift-bags, shirts.

PICNICS AND PROGRAMS

Picnic area open to the public? Yes.

Special events or wine-related programs? Anderson Valley Barrel Tasting in June. Priority Release Program includes wine shipments, discounts, and new releases.

DEMURE AND UNDERSTATED, HUSCH VINEYARDS IS A SECURE family-owned winery with a benevolent presence. While locals debate at dinner about who planted the first grapes, the official consensus is that Husch is the oldest of the modern wineries in Anderson Valley. Tony and Gretchen Husch are credited with planting their grapes in 1968; they first produced wine in 1971.

By 1973, the barn-like winery next to the tasting room had been completed and all the wine-making equipment was in place. Six years later the Husches sold the winery to Hugo Oswald, a grape grower from the east side of Mendocino County, near Talmage. His La Ribera Ranch is the namesake for Husch's popular red and white table wines. The white wines are made at the Ranch; the red wines are made here on a beautifully hilly stretch not far from the redwood forests.

Husch's rough-hewn tasting room resembles the original dwellings of homesteaders who first settled the region. It was actually once a chicken coop and a granary for storing animal feed. There's always a shady place to park under the surrounding trees. The residence, nestled behind foliage next to the vineyards, was built in the 1920s by the Nunn family, who raised sheep here for decades. From the tasting room, laughter and the clinking of glasses mean the warm Husch hospitality is being shared as usual. The rose arbor over the entry blazes a brilliant red contrast against the dark wood. Stepping through it, I am greeted by Linda or Betty or another cheerful employee and feel like I've come home.

So do the four other people at the bar. A taste of the Sauvignon Blanc is poured, someone extols the wonders of the Pinot Noir, and a honeymoon couple has a sample of the reserve Cabernet. We exchange hellos, remark about the warm day, and become an extended family in no time. Husch is known for excellent Chardonnay and Cabernet, but another success comes with its Chenin Blanc. As if on cue, a couple cruise into the tasting room and ask for a couple of bottles of it. They have brought a picnic to enjoy with friends at the source of their favorite wine, which is slightly sweet (.2% residual sugar) and tropical-tasting; perfect with the pâté and lunch meats I see in their basket.

A vineyard tour is a must when visiting Husch. The fifteen-minute stroll to the top of the knoll around which Gewürztraminer and Chardonnay vines are planted is guided by a brochure. While vines are the focus, the Sterling Silver Rose bushes planted at the end of each row are first to capture my attention.

The vineyards look different every season. In late March and April, when the buds are just forming, you can see the pruning techniques. At the same time, English daisies pop up on the gentle slopes and California poppies just begin their summer-long bloom. Later in the summer, this tour provides an up-close look at the clusters of ripening grapes. The brochure explains how the different pruning styles facilitate ripening. You may see vineyard workers pulling off leaves to expose more of the grapes to the all-important sun. In this part of the wine country, summer mornings often start with a spell of coastal fog. Keeping the grapes open to air and light is important so they don't mildew.

At the top of the knoll you have the option of walking down the other side to get a better view of the Pinot Noir, as well as more Chardonnay and Gewürztraminer, vines sloping southwest toward the Navarro River. A pause here allows a survey of the contours of the classic California coastal hills on either side. There is also a remarkable view of neighboring Roederer Estate, just across the road. On the return walk it's apparent that there isn't as much dust here as in many vineyards. That's because the weeds between the rows are mowed rather than rototilled. Besides keeping the dust down, cutting the weeds rather than digging them up helps prevent soil erosion.

Back at the tasting room, farewells are in order. After being made so welcome, it would be rude to leave without saying "so long," and purchasing some wine is a way to prolong the experience. When it's uncorked at home, it becomes another reminder of this hospitable winery with a demure facade. There's no place like Husch.

JEPSON VINEYARDS,
WINERY, AND DISTILLERY

10400 South Highway 101
Ukiah, CA 95482
(707) 468-8936
fax (707) 468-0362
Winemaker: Kurt Lorenzi
Winery owners: Robert and
Alice Jepson

ACCESS

Location: On Highway 101,
3 miles north of Hopland,
8 miles south of Ukiah.

Hours open for visits and tastings:
10:00 A.M.–5:00 P.M. daily, except
Thanksgiving, Christmas Day,
New Year's Day.

Appointment necessary for tour? Yes.

Wheelchairs accommodated? Yes.

TASTINGS

Charge for tasting? No.

Typical wines offered: Blanc de Blanc
sparkling wine, Sauvignon Blanc,
Chardonnay, French Colombard;
alembic pot still brandy.

Sales of wine-related items?
Yes, including wine glasses, T-shirts,
jewelry, and note cards.

PICNICS AND PROGRAMS

Picnic area open to the public? Yes.

Special events or wine-related programs? April: Spring Passport Open
House and Barrel Tasting. October:
Hopland Halloween Harvest Fest (in
costume!).

FANS OF WHITE WINE ARE SURE TO BE ENTHRALLED AT JEPSON. When they started the winery in 1985, owner Robert Jepson and winemaker Kurt Lorenzi acknowledged their location as a perfect growing situation for Chardonnay, Sauvignon Blanc, French Colombard, and most recently, Viognier grapes. They decided to specialize in capturing the wonders and possibilities of these white wine grapes.

On the tasting list are *methode champenoise* all-Chardonnay sparklers, Chardonnay, and Sauvignon Blanc still wines, and alembic-distilled brandy made strictly from French Colombard.

Jepson is located between Hopland and Ukiah along a straight stretch of Highway 101, also known as the Redwood Highway. When heading south, the winery is easy to reach by making a right turn into the driveway, marked by a white framed gateway. Driving north, however, caution must be taken when turning left across the highway. The imposing country Victorian on the southern knoll on the other side of the gate is now the winery office. Locals remember when it was a restaurant and a site for catered events. Before that the

property was one of the oldest sheep ranches in the county. The gravel road to the right leads to the tasting room and winery. Stay alert, for the resident peacock may be strutting along the way.

Jepson has one of the friendliest tasting rooms in the wine country. A beautifully crafted redwood ceiling and bar stand out in the white room, where cases of wine and wine-related gift items are displayed. The usual competition medals and critical reviews hang behind the bar, above the selection of wines and brandies. Several of the brandy bottles are emblazoned with the name of General Norman Schwartzkopf, of Gulf War fame. He is a personal friend of the Jepsons and a stalwart fan of their brandy, of which selected bottles are labeled with his likeness and imprimatur.

Tours are available if the tasting room isn't busy or an appointment has been made in advance. At slow times in the winter, the staff is often found in the winery anyway. One of the duties of the tasting-room staff is to riddle the 350 cases of sparkling wine. It takes an experienced hand, like tasting room manager Denise's, about forty-five minutes to riddle all the wine. Rather than do it all at once, however, she usually rotates the bottles the requisite quarter turn a few rows at a time, then tends to other business in the tasting room and returns to the winery to rotate another several rows. The complete job, in which all the spent yeast particles form at the end of the neck, takes two to three weeks. Jepson's ten-year anniversary sparkling wine, which spent nine years on its yeast, took six weeks of hand riddling.

Passing through the winery warehouse, you'll see stainless steel fermenting tanks, aging barrels, and miles of hoses—familiar sights in any winery. Unique to Jepson because it makes brandy, is the spectacular copper still, housed in an adjacent building. The French-made alembic still looks more like an art object or something from *Aladdin* than a piece of machinery. A hand-drawn diagram in front of it illustrates the distilling process for making premium cognac-style brandy.

By gently heating wine, which in this case is made only from French Colombard, a traditional Cognac grape, the vapors, or essence, and the alcohol rise into the crooked neck of the vessel and drop down into the adjoining copper container. As the vapor cools, it condenses back into liquid and contains approximately 30 percent alcohol. The meticulous process is then repeated, and after the second distillation, the resulting clear liquid is known as *eau de vie*. It is transferred into small oak barrels fabricated in the Limousin region of France. After a minimum of six years in the barrel, from which the brandy receives color, age, and flavor, it is blended, bottled, and labeled. This process of distillation, known as alembic, is the same way the finest French cognacs are made.

Back in the tasting room, the sparkling and still white wines are opened for sampling. Fruit-rich with tight bubbles, the sparkling wine is a local favorite. So is Jepson's dry, aromatic Sauvignon Blanc. If you look through the windows, you can see the 110 acres of white wine vineyards across the highway. The whole ranch encompasses 1,240 acres bounded by the Russian River to the east and the Mendocino coastal range to the west. Only the busy highway interrupts the serenity of this winery with a mission to make the most of its white wine grapes.

MᴄDᴏᴡᴇʟʟ Vᴀʟʟᴇʏ Vɪɴᴇʏᴀʀᴅs

3811 Highway 175
P.O. Box 449
Hopland, CA 95449
(707) 744-1053
fax: (707) 744-1826
e-mail: mcdowell@pacific.net
Web page:
http://www.pacific.net/~mcdowell
Winemaker: Bill Crawford
Winery owner: Keehn/Crawford
Family

ACCESS

Location: From Highway 101 in Hopland, turn east on Highway 175 for 3.8 miles, turn right at the white fence.

Hours open for visits and tastings: By appointment.

Appointment necessary for tour? Yes.

Wheelchairs accommodated? Yes.

TASTINGS

Charge for tasting? No.

Typical wines offered: Chardonnay, Marsanne, Sauvignon Blanc, Viognier; Grenache Rose; Cabernet Sauvignon, Syrah; Syrah Port.

Sales of wine-related items? Yes, including logo glasses, shirts, hats, corkscrews.

PICNICS AND PROGRAMS

Picnic area open to the public? Yes.

Special events or wine-related programs? Hopland Passport, 3rd weekend in April. Call for schedule of other events. Wine may be ordered by e-Mail and from McDowell's Web site.

MᴄDᴏᴡᴇʟʟ Vᴀʟʟᴇʏ Vɪɴᴇʏᴀʀᴅs ɪs ᴡᴇʟʟ ᴋɴᴏᴡɴ ɪɴ California as a pioneer in planting and bottling Rhone varietals. This fame, the family who owns the vineyards would say, comes courtesy of the Mediterranean climate of their valley. A closer look reveals that the Keehn, Crawford, and other resident families are as integral to each other as they are to the biodynamics of running this five-hundred-acre ranch.

In 1970, members of the Keehn/Crawford clan took over the old ranch owned in the 1900's by the Buckmans, descendants of Paxton McDowell, the valley's namesake. Five Crawford children were raised here and two still live and work the vineyards along with their families and the families of the vineyard manager and foreman. "Seamless" is the word company president Bill Crawford uses to describe the interrelationships of family, farm, food, vines, and land. Bill and spouse Vicky and their three children live here. It's always a busy place. In addition to farm chores like fence scraping and vine pruning, extracurricular activities abound. Horseback riding, waterskiing, hunting, and fishing are a few of the sports. Roping, learning to drive, and respect for the environment are rites of passage.

In 1993, the Keehn/Crawford family sold their fifteen-year-old winery production facility to concentrate on raising their grapes and children. They had built the first solar-powered winery in the United States, something they still commemorate with the blazing sun logo on the wine label. McDowell wines are still made in the building across the road, which can be part of the tour if you are interested, but the emphasis here is on the vineyards, sustainable agriculture, and organic farming. The best way to tour is to make an appointment with Bill or one of the other employees.

As he takes you through the vineyards, Bill shares his enthusiasm for organic growing like a kid who wants to show you his latest experiment. To him going organic is "more fun, more intriguing." He likes the challenge of identifying the predators—the good bugs that feast on the unwanted intruders. He is delighted with the influx of rabbits, quail, and deer that have come back. Turkeys, too. Seeing several ahead, we stop to watch as a male in full mating plumage courts several hens, who quickly spot the truck and disappear into the woods. Nonplussed, the strutting male turns his tail feathers our way and slowly folds them down before sauntering off to the woods.

Diversity is the next important aspect of organic farming, Bill points out. It is also a safeguard when planting vines. At McDowell, where Syrah and Grenache vines have grown since 1919, new plantings are done on a variety of rootstocks. On seventy-two acres at this ranch and the family's nearby Lakeview Vineyards, five clones of Syrah have been grafted on seven different rootstocks. Nineteen acres of Viognier are planted on seven rootstocks. Other varietals being raised here are Marsanne, Grenache Noir, Mourvedre, and Roussanne. The specialization in Rhone varietals was initiated when Syrah, which has become McDowell's benchmark wine, grew so well and tasted so good. "The climate and mood are Mediterranean-like," explains Bill. The similarities aren't confining, however, and he is quick to point out that while paying tribute to what they've learned from the French, in California, "we are more western—horse raisers" and are developing an independent style.

Putting the wine together with food is a big part of that style, and when the tour winds up at the tasting room, the talk switches from grape growing to wining and dining. When Bill's mother, Karen Keehn, was running the winery, McDowell became known as a leader in the pairing of wine with food. An avid cook, she was always testing things on her children as they grew up. She took that adventurousness and applied it to the nuances of wine. An easy-to-follow, sophisticated, yet unintimidating guide to wine and food produced by the winery is one of the best in the business. Without making judgments, their Rhone-style wines are described, and a list of potentially compatible foods and seasonings is provided for each varietal.

The "Sensory Perceptions" section, the most clearly written discussion of acidity, sweetness, tannin, and serving temperatures I've ever seen, describes where the perception of sweetness comes from, its affects on aroma, and how it quickly fatigues the palate. The guide also covers the origins of tannin, how its astringency interacts with the mouth, and its benefits to the longevity of wine. A companion pamphlet is a little cookbook with recipes such as Blue Cheese Corn Tamales and Crab Mold with Goat Cheese and Lemon Thyme. Some of the recipes are paired with wine suggestions and others left up to you.

One of the wine suggestions for the crab and goat cheese mold is also one of my favorite McDowell wines—Grenache Rosé. No wine has been more maligned in California than rosé, but anyone who has traveled along the Rhone in Provence knows that real rosés aren't sweet. They are dry, fruit-rich, and one of the all-time perfect companions to just about any food. Other Rhone varietals, such as Mourvèdre and Cinsault, are also being made into rosés. The grapes for McDowell's Grenache Rosé come from vines that were planted over half a century ago. The wine, with its light strawberry aroma and crisp tartness, exemplifies the best rosé has to offer.

While Bill uses the word *seamless*, I say *harmonious* describes the energy and dedication of this family of grape growers and their vineyards. Three generations and their extensions are creating a new chapter of valley history. Their Rhone varietals in the bottle and the homage to the sun on the label are only the first impressions of McDowell.

NAVARRO VINEYARDS

5601 Highway 128

P.O. Box 47

Philo, CA 95466

(800) 537-9463; (707) 895-3686

fax (707) 895-3647

Winemaker: Jim Klein

Winery owners: Deborah Cahn and Ted Bennett

ACCESS

Location: From Highway 101, take Highway 128 west about 36 miles; winery is on north side of road.

Hours open for visits and tastings: 10:00 A.M.-6:00 P.M. daily, April-October; 10:00 A.M.-5:00 P.M. daily, November-March; Closed Thanksgiving, Christmas Day, and New Year's Day.

Appointment necessary for tour? Yes.

Wheelchairs accommodated? Yes.

TASTINGS

Charge for tasting? No.

Typical wines offered: Chardonnay, Gewürztraminer, Riesling, Sauvignon Blanc; Pinot Noir; Late Harvest Riesling; plus non-alcoholic grape juices and verjus.

Sales of wine-related items? No.

PICNICS AND PROGRAMS

Picnic area open to the public? Yes.

Special events or wine-related programs? Pre-Release Tasting Program includes wine shipments; newsletter.

ONE OF THE BUSIEST TASTING ROOMS IN ANDERSON VALLEY IS also one of the oldest. Deborah Cahn and Ted Bennett bought the 910-acre ranch in 1973. A year later they planted their first Pinot Noir and Gewürztraminer vines; Chardonnay grapes followed. The Gewürztraminer has become a standard bearer for Alsatian-style wines in California, and Navarro has become one of the industry's most successful direct-marketing wineries.

The bulk of Navarro wine is sold through the tasting room and by mail order. This concept came after Bennett sold Pacific Stereo, a company he was with for fifteen years. He and Cahn moved to the country to settle into a lifestyle city dwellers only imagine. While realizing dreams means an incredible amount of work, the two do it with independence and aplomb. Their tasteful approach applies to everything from the architecture of the redwood tasting room to the quality of the wines, from the entry gate to the well-groomed flower gardens.

Navarro has such a devoted following, its fans make ritual visits to pick up or order wine. Navarro's newsletter, with its personal flair and anecdotes, encourages those who receive it to feel like part of a family. I've heard people remark that the

stories written about each wine make them want to buy a bottle so they don't feel left out.

Making an appointment for a tour means an even more personal involvement in learning about Navarro. Cahn or Bennett leads the tour and tailors the information to the group's interest. If anyone has set foot on another vineyard that day, disposable white "booties" are handed out to pull over your shoes. This is a preventative measure against phylloxera, the root louse that is devastating so many vineyards in California. The infestation may be spread by soil being transferred from one vineyard to another.

First stop on the tour is the original Gewürztraminer vineyard behind the tasting room. Navarro's dry Gewürztraminer and semi-sweet blend of Gewürztraminer and Riesling have defined the California style of these wines of the Alsatian region between France and Germany. The pruning technique here is also Alsatian-inspired. Each cane is bent back and tied, and the result resembles the heart-shaped vines seen along the Rhine in the winter. The reason for this technique is that Gewürztraminer is notorious for not producing in the middle of the vine. Turning it is a way to encourage production.

A little way up the hill are the Chardonnay vines. Here, vertical trellises allow the vines to be their own solar collectors and to stay as dry as possible during the valley's typically foggy summer mornings. The trellising exposes more grapes to the hot afternoon sun and prevents the possibility of botrytis, a mold that is undesirable on Chardonnay or Pinot Noir grapes.

At this point you have the option of jumping in the truck and driving around the property to the hillside Pinot Noir vineyard with its spectacular views of the valley. Afterward, the tour continues from the animal pasture, where curious llamas, horses, and sheep come to the fence and enjoy the attention. These are all daughter Sarah's projects, as well as "one of the joys of having a family farm."

A short walk away, the winery is housed in various buildings around the crush pad, where all the action takes place during harvest. All the harvesting at Navarro is done at night. Pickers arrive at midnight and crushing begins at seven in the morning. Picking at night, when the grapes are naturally cool,

is beneficial for the long cool fermentation that preserves the aromatics in the wine.

Being relatively small (about twenty-five thousand cases) and in charge of its own marketing allows Navarro to do things large wineries don't have time for, like producing small amounts of a single wine. Several varieties of Pinot Noir, Chardonnay, and Pinot Gris vines planted on six different rootstocks can all be made into wine individually. One of Navarro's specialties, Pinot Noir, receives the most hands-on treatment. *Methode à l'ancienne* means the wine is never pumped. During fermentation, the cap (the layer of skins and stems that rises to the surface) is pushed down by hand three times a day until the right amount of color is extracted. Then the juice is dumped, rather than pumped, into a press. This extra effort is done as a precaution to help prevent any stems and seeds from causing bitterness in the wine.

A visit to the barrel room is next. Here is where all the lots are stored and kept track of by computer. Glasses are offered to sample the differences straight from the barrels. If Bennett is available, he talks about the different oak woods and origins of the barrels. Every step of the way, the feeling is that this winery is motivated by quality more than efficiency.

The proof comes at the end of the tour when the glasses are set on the bar in the tasting room. Comparing a Chardonnay that came from a certain lot to another adds to the process of learning about what results from different techniques. Each year at least one or two irresistible blends are made in tiny quanitities, and they are often the most fun to try.

Like many of the wineries in Anderson Valley, Navarro is a picnic destination. The arbored tables in the vineyards attract couples and groups on crisp sunny days in January, when the vines are dormant spindles. They are also crowded with revelers in the heat of July, when foliage is lush and the grapes are ripening. It feels so comfortable to be here, it's not surprising so many direct sale customers keep returning.

OBESTER WINERY

9200 Highway 128
Philo, CA 95466
(800) 310-2404; (707) 895-3814

Winemaker: Bruce Regalia

Winery owners: Sandy and
Paul Obester

ACCESS

Location: From Highway 101, take
Highway 128 west for about 31 miles;
winery is on the southwest side of
the road.

Hours open for visits and tastings:
10:00 A.M.-5:00 P.M. daily. Closed
Thanksgiving, Christmas Day, New
Year's Day, and Super Bowl Sunday
when the San Francisco 49ers play.

Appointment necessary for tour? Yes.

Wheelchairs accommodated? Yes.

TASTINGS

Charge for tasting? No.

Typical wines offered: Chardonnay,
Gewürztraminer, Johannisberg
Riesling, Sauvignon Blanc; Cabernet
Sauvignon, Pinot Noir, Sangiovese,
Zinfandel; Late Harvest Riesling.

Sales of wine-related items? Yes, large
selection of flavored vinegars, olive
oil, mustards, and other condiments;
cookbooks, clothing, and logo glasses.

PICNICS AND PROGRAMS

Picnic area open to the public? Yes.

Special events or wine-related programs? June: Anderson Valley Barrel
Tasting. Adopt-A-Vine includes
adoption papers, wine, discounts,
and party.

BESTER WINERY IS FUN. THE FUN BEGINS INSIDE THE COUNTRY farmhouse tasting room with its cheery yellow paint. It continues while you taste wine from standard bottles with untraditional labels and from fancifully shaped Italian bottles. It climaxes in the vineyard, where the most fun happens with Obester's Adopt-a-Vine program.

This is not to say the serious business of winemaking is slighted. Quite the contrary. A long legacy of Italian wine-making, part of the Obester's story, is apparent around the tasting room, where remnants of Sandy Obester's ancestry are preserved. Museum-quality antique wine equipment and a photographic exhibit pay tribute to grandfather John Gemello and his brother Mario, and their winery in Mountain View, California. Sandy and Paul Obester acquired the old Gemello winery assets in 1982, after her Uncle Mario retired.

In an earlier sequence of events, grandfather John Gemello, who founded the Mountain View winery in 1934, passed on his winemaking enthusiasm to the Obesters. While Paul was still vice-president of a small electronics firm, he and Sandy began making wine in their basement under Gemello's tute-lage. In 1977, the Obesters started a small winery in an old barn in Half Moon Bay. In order to draw people to their out-of-the-way spot, they instituted a European tradition. Just like at wineries in the old countries, consumers bring their empty wine bottles and fill them straight from the barrels; this is a custom Gemello Winery carried on since its inception. Today, Obester's newsletter has a calendar listing the days wine is available at their Half Moon Bay winery.

By 1982, Sandy and Paul branched out and bought property in Anderson Valley that previously had been a truck farm with organic apple orchards. Six years later, the 1929 farmhouse was converted to a tasting room, and a metal building in back became the winery. Eight acres of Chardonnay, Pinot Noir, and Gewürz-traminer were planted in 1991, and maintaining organic status of the original farm remains a priority in the vineyards.

Winemaker Bruce Regalia also came on board in 1991. He leads tours around the property when he has the time and an appointment is made in advance, but most of the sights can be seen on your own.

In the tasting room, while taking in the exhibits, you might start by tasting the estate Gewürztraminer, a spicy, slightly sweet wine, or the fruity dry Sauvignon Blanc. Take a look at the photo exhibit showing early winemaking at the original Gemello Winery. Below it is the original press, which dates to 1897. A hand pump, a horizontal filter similar to those used today, and a basket press are all labeled for identification. In contrast to the historical display is another of the Obesters' contemporary enterprises. Flavored olive oils, vinegars, mus-tard, and other condiments, also produced by Sandy and Paul and packaged in unusual beautiful bottles, are set along one wall and on a couple of tables.

Speaking of fancy bottles, be sure to try Obester's Sangiovese in the sleek glass bottle with one flat side. This wine, made from the predominant grape used in Chianti, is rapidly gaining popularity in California. The grapes for this wine come from Hopland. Growing Sangiovese is labor intensive because it is

such a prolific producer that, to maintain quality, half of the fruit has to be knocked off. When a vine bears too much fruit, the flavor gets thin and harsh. Sangiovese is worth the effort to grow and make, according to Regalia, because it goes so well with food. He recommends it with meat and poultry, especially with pork cooked with apples.

The grapes for Obester's Zinfandel come from a seventy-year-old vineyard in Redwood Valley, a source of some of California's finest Zin. To make the wine, the grapes are lightly crushed and then fermented in one-and-a-half-ton bins. Skin contact lasts seven to ten days before the grapes are pressed. The juice is aged in oak barrels for eighteen months. Racking is done three or four times to help clarify the wine. Next is filtering and bottling.

While tasting the robust flavors of these smooth red wines, look out the window over the bar. Past the adobe pizza oven (only used by staff), where the field dips down,

two tributary creeks join to form the headwaters of the Navarro River. You can walk around outside to get a closer look and take a stroll through the vineyards, but before heading outside ask about Obester's Adopt-A-Vine program.

While the bottle shapes and friendly staff have already contributed to the light atmosphere, a trip into the vineyards next to the picnic area will have you in stitches. To put it briefly, the Obesters have put up each of their grapevines for adoption. Parents pay a fee, name their vine, and become part of a unique club with events and wine discounts as part of the package. The fun comes from reading the names of the vines. Some are serious family monikers, but most are tongue-in-cheek, like Julio Vine Glaciers, Lester Sylvester Obester, Albert Vinestein, and Pinot Envy. The grapes make good wine in spite of what their parents named them.

PARDUCCI WINE CELLARS
501 Parducci Road
Ukiah, CA 95482
(707) 462-5357
(707) 462-5358
Winemaker: William Hill
Winery owner: Hill and Thorna Wines

ACCESS

Location: From Highway 101 take the Lake Mendocino off-ramp immediately north of Ukiah; coming from the south turn left at the bottom of the off-ramp and follow the signs.

Hours open for visits and tastings: 9:00 A.M.-5:00 P.M. daily. Closed Easter, Thanksgiving, Christmas Day, New Year's Day.

Appointment necessary for tour? Yes.

Wheelchairs accommodated? Yes.

TASTINGS

Charge for tasting? No.

Typical wines offered: Chardonnay, Sauvignon Blanc, Vintage White, Gewürztraminer; White Zinfandel; Cabernet Sauvignon, Gamay Beaujolais, Merlot, Petite Sirah, Pinot Noir, Vintage Red, Zinfandel.

Sales of wine-related items? Yes, including logo glasses, books, clothing, and food products.

PICNICS AND PROGRAMS

Picnic area open to the public? Yes.

Special events or wine related programs? Food and Wine programs. Call the winery for schedules.

MENDOCINO'S OLDEST CONTINUOUSLY RUNNING WINERY is the only one in the county with regularly scheduled tours. The tour includes an introduction to winemaking and a historical account similar to those of other Italian winemakers, who bestowed a rich heritage upon California's wine history.

Adolph Parducci came to America from Tuscany when he was 16 years old. He started his first winery in Cloverdale, thirty miles south of Ukiah. A fire and then Prohibition forced its closure. Undaunted, he bought property in Mendocino County in 1921 and planted vineyards on his "Home Ranch." While Prohibition forbade the public sale of wine, it didn't thwart the Italian wine tradition. In fact, in some places winemaking actually thrived, particularly since sacramental wine was needed for the Church. Households were allowed to have one hundred gallons of wine a year—and someone had to make it. By 1931, signs pointed to the end of Prohibition, and by 1932 Adolph Parducci had constructed his winery. The next year Prohibition was officially repealed.

Tours begin in the tasting room, spaciously housed in an Italian-inspired hacienda. The family home and other buildings are nestled against a hillside. "Everything is built for gravity flow of the juice and wine," says the guide. Crushing and fermenting is done at the top of the slope, which lets the wine flow downhill to barrels and bottling.

On the way to the crush pad, the walk is lined by a beautiful lichen-covered stone retainer wall built by Adolph and his four sons in the 1940s. As you proceed, the guide discusses Prohibition, the number of vineyards planted, and how much wine was made and moved around illegally. He points to the cellar under the original family residence where wine barrels were kept and where townspeople brought their jugs and bottles to be filled.

The crush pad features an impressive display of ten- to thirty-thousand-gallon stainless steel tanks under a huge metal roof. White grapes are processed on one side and red on the other. Mammoth crushers line the outer wall on each side, while the huge tanks with glycol jackets cool the juice for fermentation. Seeds and stems from crushing, called *pomace*, are mixed with rice hulls ("a tradition from the old days") and used to mulch the vineyards.

While the tanks, crushers, and presses on this level are similar to those found at any modern winery, in the next building down the hill is a scene that was state of the art in the 1930s. Outside, overhead pipes transport the wine into the old structure, heavily stuccoed for insulation and bordered by some of the winery's fifty- to sixty-year old Cabernet Sauvignon vines. Inside are more stainless tanks, the filtering systems, and then, the prize view: a room full of seventeen- to twenty-thousand-gallon tanks fabricated from vertical grain virgin redwood. These redwood tanks have a beautiful shiny patina, due in part to their beeswax sealant. Red wines with Parducci's label start out with some time in the redwood tanks and then are transferred to American or French oak barrels.

The cellar was built a few stairs underground to keep it cool. Sixteen beautiful tanks line each side of the aisle. Cellar records on each tank keep track of the kind of grape inside, when it was picked, when racked, and when the tank was topped. One tank is full of Carignane, an old Italian varietal often called the "work horse" grape because of its prolific growth and excellence for blending.

The next room is filled with new redwood vats. These are twenty feet tall, hold 4,200 gallons, and don't yet have the patina of their aged counterparts. Further along, six small oak barrels hold Port, made in years when Zinfandel grapes hang on the vine long enough and conditions are right for the sweet botrytis yeast to attack them.

The tour finishes with a walk through the picnic area, around which trunks of table grape vines extend ten feet up to form a trellised arbor. The gnarly old vines around the tasting room produce Palomino grapes, used in Spain for making sherry. Inside, at the tasting bar, current vintages of Chardonnay, Pinot Noir, and Merlot can be tasted. The old and the new blend comfortably here. At Parducci, the reverence for things past enhances the tastes of wines present.

REDWOOD VALLEY CELLARS

7051 North State Street
P.O. Box 805
Redwood Valley, CA 95470
(707) 485-0322
fax (707) 485-6784

Winemaker: David Rosenthal

Winery owners: Charlie and Martha Barra and family, Bill and Janet Pauli and family.

ACCESS

Location: From Highway 101, take the West Road exit to the north; turn right at the first intersection and continue for 2 miles.

Hours open for visits and tastings: 9:00 A.M.-6:00 P.M. daily, May-October; 9:00 A.M.-5:00 P.M. daily, November-April. Closed Thanksgiving, Christmas Day, and New Year's Day.

Appointment necessary for tour? Yes.

Wheelchairs accommodated? Yes.

TASTINGS

Charge for tasting? No.

Typical wines offered: Chardonnay, Merlot, Cabernet Sauvignon; plus releases from a number of other Mendocino wineries, including Braren-Pauli, Redwood Valley Cellars, Elizabeth Vineyards, Whaler Vineyards, Domaine St. Gregory, Monte Volpe, Claudia Springs, Duncan Peak, Pacific Star, and McDowell Valley Vineyards.

Sales of wine-related items? Yes, large inventory of Mendocino-made foodstuffs, condiments, preserves, and products.

PICNICS AND PROGRAMS

Picnic area open to the public? Yes.

Special events or wine-related programs? Taste of Redwood Valley, Father's Day Weekend in June; call for schedule of other events.

ONE WAY TO SAMPLE THE WINES OF SEVERAL MENDOCINO producers at the same time is by stopping at the Redwood Valley Cellars tasting room. It sounds unusual to share space with other wineries, but the partners in this venture are exceptional. The Barras and the Paulis come from two of the county's oldest agricultural families and have spent decades promoting local products. At this tasting room they are committed to bringing as many Mendocino County wines and foods as possible together under one roof. What a roof it is!

You can see the distinctive building from Highway 101 about ten miles north of Ukiah. Modeled after an inverted champagne glass, the roof rises to its stem above the circular brick and redwood building. Behind it are some of the biggest wine-storage containers in the business. Once known by the locals as the "tank farm," the winery was built in 1971 by Weibel, a Mission San Jose winery. Charlie and Martha Barra and Bill and Janet Pauli bought the property in 1995. "We could have made it only our own, but I don't work that way," says Charlie Barra. "The wines that go out of Mendocino are all unique and different. This gives consumers a chance to see what a good job Mendocino wineries do."

Charlie's family came from northern Italy in the early 1900s. Both his parents had worked in vineyards in Europe, and his father worked as a waiter at the Palace Hotel in San Francisco before coming to Mendocino County.

Barra has been part of the Mendocino wine industry since World War II, when he was in high school and leased his own vineyard at age sixteen. In the 1930s and 1940s, most of California's wine grapes were produced for bulk Burgundy and White Chablis, but Charlie, being an innovative spirit, planted varietals—Pinot Noir, Pinot Blanc, Riesling, and Chardonnay—in the 1950s. Barra's vineyards are on 150 acres about two miles north of the tasting room. He sold the grapes for thirty years to Wente Brothers Winery in Livermore. Now, he sells the grapes to Fetzer, Beringer, and other wineries, and with some of his grapes, he makes wine with the Redwood Valley Cellars label. He and Bill Pauli bought this facility when they heard the previous owners were selling it and saw it as an opportunity to expand the visibility of Mendocino wines.

In addition to working with Charlie, Bill is half the partnership in Braren-Pauli Winery, which produces twelve to fifteen thousand cases of super-premium varietals a year. Their wines were made previously at other facilities, but with the purchase of Redwood Valley Cellars, the upgrading of the winery means that production of their Mendocino Chardonnay, Mendocino Merlot, and Mendocino Cabernet Sauvignon is being done here.

Bill is the fourth generation of his family to be born and raised in nearby Potter Valley. In the early years, his family had dairy cows and pears on the property and fished commercially on the coast. His wife Janet's family came to the county in 1868. The Pauli family ranch, originally fifteen acres, is now 450. Their grapes, including Chardonnay, Sauvignon Blanc,

Semillon, Johannisberg Riesling, and Pinot Noir, are used for their own winery venture rather than for Redwood Valley Cellars wine. Pears still grow on nine acres.

The entrance to the tasting room is around the side, just next to a large picnic area shaded by valley oaks and magnolia trees. The interior of the tasting room was remodeled by the Barras and Paulis to create the light, open space you see today. Every time you stop, something is going on.

Part of that is due to the energy of Martha Barra. Her vision of the tasting room being a showcase of Mendocino food and wine includes having frequent events here. It is a good source of condiments and preserves made by Mendocino's cottage producers. One of these, Russian River Pistachios, is a neighbor on adjacent acreage to the south.

Redwood Valley Cellars is the place to learn about Braren-Pauli and Redwood Valley Cellars wines, as well as about some of the wineries that are too small to staff tasting rooms. Elizabeth Vineyards, for example, produces Zinfandel, Chardonnay, and Sauvignon Blanc wine not too far away in Redwood Valley. Russ and Ann Nyborg's Whaler Vineyards' Zinfandel is locally renowned. Italian varietals, raised in Mendocino, such as Nebbiolo, Sangiovese, and Sesso (which means sexy) by Greg Graziano's Monte Volpe, are available for tasting. As are Grazziano's Domaine St. Gregory Burgundian-style Pinot Blanc and Pinot Noir.

With so many wineries represented, this is one of the best places in the county to pick up a delectable sampling of the wide range of wine, as well as food, produced in Mendocino.

ROEDERER ESTATE

ROEDERER ESTATE

4501 Highway 128
Philo, CA 95466
(707) 895-2288
fax (707) 895-2120

Winemaker: Michel Salgues

Winery owner: Jean-Claude Rouzaud,
Champagne Louis Roederer

ACCESS

Location: From Highway 101,
take Highway 128 west and drive
38 miles.

Hours open for visits and tastings:
11:00 A.M.-5:00 P.M. daily, except
Thanksgiving and Christmas Day.

Appointment necessary for tour? Yes.

Wheelchairs accommodated? Yes.

TASTINGS

Charge for tasting? Yes, $3.00
applied to purchase.

Typical wines offered: Brut, Brut Rose,
and Hermitage sparkling wine.

Sales of wine-related items? No.

PICNICS AND PROGRAMS

Picnic area open to the public? No.

Special events or wine-related programs? June: Anderson Valley Barrel
Tasting. Mail order available.

ROEDERER ESTATE CONVEYS TWO IMPRESSIONS: FIRST CLASS and French. The setting, alone, reminds me of rural France. The fruit and vegetable stands down the road are like Saturday morning village markets. The proximity of farm animals and orchards to vineyards and the size of the many family-owned wineries in Anderson Valley is also similar. Of course there are differences. Gigantic stands of redwoods like those just to the west are only found in California, and Roederer's building is built of redwood, not stone. Yet, from the turn up the sweeping driveway to entering the tasting room and sipping the first sparkling wine, I feel immersed in the best of the French style.

In some ways, it's only what you'd expect knowing that the parent company, House of Champagne Louis Roederer, has been a family-owned winery since it was founded in 1776. Louis Rouzaud took over the helm in 1979 from his grandmother, Madame Olry-Roederer, who ran the company for the previous forty years. In addition to consistently fine French champagne, Louis Roederer makes Cristal, which sets the world's standard as the epitome of champagne.

When the company looked for a place to expand its holdings, it sent scouts to research several parts of the world. The decision to locate in Mendocino County was based on the soil, the climate, and the taste of the grapes and wine from Anderson Valley. In 1981, the first estate grapes were planted, and the winery was completed in 1986. The forty-eight-thousand-square-foot facility is settled unobtrusively into the hill above the roadside Pinot Noir vines.

Inside the tasting room, high ceilings, French fabrics, and the polished 250-year-old floor tiles, which came from the Bordeaux region, are *á la mode française*. The framed engravings on the wall, depicting the old ways of winemaking, are from an antique French book on Louis Roederer. Floor-to-ceiling windows capture the magnificent view and setting. The pewter-topped bar, from an old Parisian cafe, once had a gutter on one side to catch spills. The tasting glasses are made by one of France's finest glassware companies, Crystalline.

A tour of the winery doesn't erase its French-ness, especially if winemaker Michel Salgues is the guide. While the facility is ultra-modern and state-of-the-art, the serious approach to winemaking is softened by Salgues' charming manner, twinkling eyes, and very French accent. We begin at the crush pad, on the lower level behind the building. Beyond are 155 acres of Pinot Noir and Chardonnay, the typical grapes for making sparkling wine. Roederer Estate grows more grapes than needed for its own production, which means they choose the best of the crop for making wine for the *cuvée*, or base wine. They also blend *cuvée* from different years to produce their non-vintage brut. The best wine in an exceptional year is reserved for making Roederer Estate's *tête de cuvée*, or top of the line, which they call Hermitage. In 1990, only three percent of the wine was Hermitage quality; the vintage was extolled by such luminaries in the wine press as Anthony Dias Blue, who said it was "maybe the best bubbly ever made in the United States."

One word, *finesse*, is repeated throughout the tour. It applies to the meticulous hand-picking and sorting of grapes, the extremely gentle pressing, carefully monitored fermentation, and ultimately the artful blending. In the end, the bubbles define *finesse*.

One highlight on the tour comes as soon as we walk up the hill and into the back door of the winery. From the dark hallway, we look through a large window at the dimly lit barrel room. Four of the 1,100-gallon casks are illuminated to show the beautiful carvings of vineyard scenes on the ends. These motifs were also taken from the old French book on Roederer.

My favorite experience on the tour is when Salgues disgorges a bottle of sparkling wine by hand. At one time, hand-disgorging was the only way to remove the plug of spent yeast that gathers in the bottle during its sparkling fermentation. Now it's done by machine. *A la mode ancienne* (for old-times sake), Salgues demonstrates how it used to be done. It is no simple feat to knock the cap off the bottle and release the coagulated plug, losing as little of the sparkling wine as possible. His masterful touch leaves less than an inch of its contents missing. Along the wall are two of the world's biggest mechanized riddling machines. Made in France, each holds 480 cases—5,760 bottles—and takes five to six days, turning the wine three times a day, to bring the residue to the neck of

the bottle. Hand riddling takes around two weeks.

After the low illumination of the cellar, the overhead windows and bright lights of the bottling room are dazzling. The din of machinery fills the room while bottles are automatically disgorged, topped, corked, and capped. Employees stand by to catch low-fills or any other less-than-perfect bottles.

A long narrow hallway leads back to the tasting room, where the Brut, Brut Rose, and Hermitage sparkling wines are sampled. Taking a sip of the Hermitage, I am struck by the fragrance of the little dancing bubbles, each one singular and crisp. I notice the long finish of the wine across my tongue and all the way down; it feels like drinking a cloud.

With flute in hand, I walk to the windows and sit at the cafe table to admire this hilltop panorama of vines below and redwoods in the distance. It's difficult to leave, but I must. Setting my flute on the bar, in my best accent I sing out "*au revoir*" as I go out the door. That's what they do in France.

SCHARFFENBERGER CELLARS

8501 Highway 128
Philo, CA 95466
(707) 895-2957
fax (707) 895-2758
Winemaker: Willis Tex Sawyer
Winery owner: Louis Vuitton Moët Hennessey, France;
John Scharffenberger, founder.

ACCESS

Location: In the town of Philo on the northwest end, about 35 miles west of Highway 101, 22 miles east of Highway 1.

Hours open for visits and tastings: 11:00 A.M.-5:00 P.M. daily. Closed Thanksgiving, Christmas Day, New Year's Day.

Appointment necessary for tour? Yes.

Wheelchairs accommodated? Yes.

TASTINGS

Charge for tasting? Yes, $3.00 applicable to purchase.

Typical wines offered: Brut, Brut Rosé, Crémant sparkling wines. Chardonnay, Pinot Noir, Pinot Meunier, and Syrah at various times.

Sales of wine-related items? Yes, including logo glassses, shirts, and corkscrews.

PICNICS AND PROGRAMS

Picnic area open to the public? Yes.

Special events or wine-related programs? Art exhibits and opening receptions; Anderson Valley Barrel Tasting in June; Holiday Open House; musical and other events in the redwood grove. Box picnic lunches. Call the winery for a schedule.

THERE ARE SEVERAL WAYS TO VISIT SCHARFFENBERGER Cellars, on the edge of tiny downtown Philo. With its own grove of redwoods, this winery is a destination that makes picnicking a must, whether you pack your own or call ahead and order a catered box lunch from the winery. The winery tour, by appointment only, provides a comprehensive description of how the flavor and bubbles get into a bottle of sparkling wine. Spontaneous visits anytime provide an opportunity to enjoy the hospitality of the tasting room.

While sipping a glass of bubbly from the tasting room, you can mosey out to the porch of the white farmhouse bungalow or wander the front room and study the current art being exhibited. When a new show is hung, you're welcome to attend the weekend reception, a great event for hobnobbing with residents from Anderson Valley, as well as with art lovers from inland and coastal Mendocino County.

The winery, a grandly scaled thirty-five-thousand square-foot facility, is behind the tasting room. Its design is spacious enough both for the easy passing of two forklifts and so the winemaker's truck can be driven from one end to the other (a feature pointed out on the tour). Architectural details such as the spun-steel light sconces, the sandblasted glass entry to the private entertaining quarters, and the maple railing add artistic touches. The tour begins just inside the riveted metal double doors, where a raised walkway mezzanine overlooks the cavernous bottling and riddling room. If he's not occupied with other duties, the winemaker himself, Tex Sawyer, will be your guide.

The first stop, on an outdoor balcony at the corner of the crush pad, is where it all begins. Here, Chardonnay and Pinot Noir grapes, all handpicked in Anderson Valley and most from the fifty-six acres you see around the winery, arrive in half-ton bins. The winery's founder, John Scharffenberger, was one of the first to recognize the potential of Anderson Valley grapes for making champagne style—*methode champenoise*—sparkling wine. In 1981, he was the first to produce it commercially.

As California's coolest wine-growing region, Anderson Valley is similar to the Champagne region in France. It is only ten degrees lower in latitude than Champagne; the mean temperature in Champagne is fifty-three degrees; here it is fifty-six. The lower latitude and slightly warmer temperature mean longer days of sunlight. As Tex describes Anderson Valley's advantages, he says, "France gets a great vintage based on perfect growing conditions every ten to twelve years, while we get it every year."

Maximizing the flavor of the fruit is the goal in Scharffenberger's style of winemaking. During harvest, you can watch the grapes being dropped into the bladder press, designed especially for making champagne-style wine. The first gentle pressing produces the clearest, pure juice from the grapes and is used for the *cuvée* for Scharffenberger's sparkling wines. The pressure is then increased by a small amount, and a second pressing, known as "first taille," produces juice, a small amount of which is used for the sparkling wines and the rest sold to other wineries. An optional third, slightly harder squeezing makes what is known in the business as *ribeche*, which is sold to other wineries, where, after fermentation, it becomes a blending component eventually mixed with other wine. Every batch of juice is kept separate and labeled by vineyard and variety, as well as by which pressing it came from.

Moving back into the winery, the tour follows the wine's flow. The juice for *cuvée* rests overnight, then is racked into the stainless steel fermenters in this room and mixed with yeast. After primary fermentation the wine goes into another fermentation known as malolactic. "We used to be the only ones using malolactic in our sparkling wine, but other wineries have seen the benefits. This strain of bacteria knocks out the corners and makes the wine smooth and round, giving it a creamy vanilla character," says Tex. The process takes six to eight weeks.

In February and March, blending takes place in two 21,000-gallon tanks. The huge size of the tanks helps maintain consistency. Aromas characteristic of wine from Anderson Valley include apple and floral from the Chardonnay and strawberry, plum, and roses from the Pinot Noir.

The finished wine is transported back into the room where the tour began. All the bottling processes take place here. Once bottled and capped with a crown bottle cap, the wine is stored on its lees, or yeast. The bubbles develop during the first six

weeks, but the bottles are stored for two to three years, a period known as *tirage*. At the end of *tirage*, the bottles are transferred to riddling bins and placed on automated riddling racks. Each rack holds 336 cases of wine; the bottles, placed neck in flange, are rotated several times a day to move the residual yeast to the neck.

Wine is bottled from March through May, but disgorging takes place throughout the year. Transferred from the riddling racks, the bottles are placed upside down and their necks are frozen. The bottles are righted, and as soon as the bottle cap is removed, the frozen residue is forced out (disgorged) by the pressure from the bubbles inside. A dosage of sugar and wine replaces the lost liquid, and the bottle is corked. Once the cork is in, the bottle is kept for three months before it goes to market to allow the flavors to come back into balance.

At this point the topic turns to consumption. The best time to drink sparkling wine is soon after purchasing it. The flavors are purer within its first year, after which they change

and get an older, sometimes oxidized, taste. The two enemies to sparkling wine are light and heat. The dark green bottles help deter light from interfering with flavor and changing the wine's color. Maintaining the wine at a constant temperature throughout its production, as well as after it is in the bottle, is also important. Once you bring a bottle of sparkling wine home, if you put it in the refrigerator leave it there until it's time to drink it.

With this practical piece of information revealed, the tour ends with the departure through the riveted doors and back to the tasting room. Just before the old weathered barn is a graveled road that leads to Scharffenberger's twelve-hundred-year-old redwood grove. It's worth the walk through the vineyards to see this magnificent stand of trees. Picnickers come here to stretch out in the meadow or sit at a table and dine from their baskets. This is also the site of musical and theatrical events hosted by the winery. These, too, are lures to visit Scharffenberger and enjoy a picnic, the perfect meal with a bottle of sparkling wine?

BRANDY DISTILLERY
GERMAIN-ROBIN ALAMBIC, INC.

GERMAIN-ROBIN ALAMBIC, INC.

P.O. Box 175
Ukiah, CA 95482
Business office:
3001 South State Street #31
Ukiah, CA 95482
(707) 462-0314; (707) 462-3221
fax (707) 462-8103

Brandy maker: Hubert Germain-Robin

Winery owners: Ansley Coale, Hubert
Germain-Robin, et al.

ACCESS

Location: Business and Retail: from
Highway 101, take the South State
Street offramp and turn north onto
State Street. The office is on the right
in a group of warehouses.
Ranch Distillery: Call for directions.

Hours open for visits and tastings:
By appointment.

Appointment necessary for tour? Yes.

Wheelchairs accommodated? At the
business and retail office only.

TASTINGS

Charge for tasting? No tasting.

Typical brandies offered: Fine (VSOP);
Shareholder's Blend; Christmas Blend
(100 cases only); Select Barrel XO;
Single Barrels; Cigar Blend; Grappa of
Zinfandel; Cabernet/Petite Sirah or
Muscat Mistelles; 10-liter casks.

Sales of wine-related items? Yes,
antique French tools at the ranch.
Retail sales also at Dunnewood
Winery, Scharffenberg Cellars, Fetzer
Vineyards.

PICNICS AND PROGRAMS

Picnic area open to the public? No.

Special events or wine-related
programs? No.

O F ALL OF MENDOCINO'S GASTRONOMIC ATTRACTIONS, Germain-Robin's cognac-style brandy distillery has the most fortuitous story. In 1981, Hubert and Carole Germain-Robin, two young French travelers, were hitch-hiking in northern California when they were picked up by Ansley Coale, owner of a two-thousand-acre ranch west of Ukiah. Ansley invited the Germain-Robins to visit. At the time, he was contemplating giving up his job teaching ancient history at the University of California in Berkeley to live full-time on his ranch. Hubert was exploring the possibility of establishing an American location to get back into the business his family had been in since 1782. He came from one of the oldest artisanal houses of Cognac, but it had been swallowed up by the house of Martell. Seeing limited opportunities in France to continue the craft of his ancestors, he was checking out the possibilities in other parts of the world. Call their meeting serendipity or fate.

Within a year, Hubert had located a beautiful old still in an abandoned distillery in a small village near Cognac. He shipped it to Ansley's ranch, and he and Carole moved to Mendocino County. After cleaning the still and building a brick base underneath, Hubert distilled enough wine into brandy to fill fourteen barrels with Germain-Robin's first vintage. It would be four years before the first hundred cases would be bottled in 1987. (Out of respect to French protocol, just like with champagne, we don't call it cognac because it isn't made in Cognac.)

An appointment is necessary to visit the distillery, but seeing the artisanal approach to making a fine brandy is like paying homage to the source. What a source it is!

After a long bumpy ride from Ukiah, the last stretch winds up the unmarked driveway to the quiet solitude of Eagle Rock Ranch. An occasional bird flies over. Billowing clouds float over the grassy, oak tree–dotted hilltop. The location is about as far from Cognac as you can get, but so are some of the approaches of this New World enterprise.

The hands-on alembic distillation process is the same here as in France. (Germain-Robin uses the French spelling, alambic, in their name.) Differences begin with the grapes and the wines Hubert uses. Traditionally, Ugni Blanc (also known as Trebbiano) is made into the base wine for Cognac. Seeing the palate of possibilities grown in Mendocino, Hubert broke tradition. While using some French Colombard, another typical brandy grape, he also selects and directs the winemaking of base wines made from Semillon, Chenin Blanc, and even the red Gamay Beaujolais and Pinot Noir grapes. His philosophy is that premium wine produces a superior product.

Distillation is done between August and February. That's when the action in the distillery, which from the outside looks like any of the other redwood farm buildings, is the highest. Three hundred gallons of wine go into the onion-domed pot. It is gently heated to allow the alcohol to rise as steam and collect in the curved copper swan's-neck tubing. The process continues over a ten-hour period, and as the vapors are cooled they slowly descend and condense into about 110 gallons of cloudy liquid called *brouillis*. A second distillation, using three hundred gallons of *brouillis*, takes twelve hours following the same process, but it results in a clear *eau-de-vie*, or fresh brandy, which is transferred to oak barrels. The flavor at this point is light with floral aromas. Color comes from aging in oak barrels.

A few feet away from the distillery is the barrel-filled cellar. The barrels are made of Limousin oak in Cognac by the "last guy who air dries the oak," a process that takes four to five years. When the barrels are new they have the strongest impact, so the fresh brandies stay in them only about eleven months. Afterward they are transferred from barrel to barrel for control and consistency. Fresh out of the still, the alcoholic content is about 70 percent. Rainwater is collected, filtered, and added in small increments to bring it down to 40 percent.

Some wines are left as single barrels and vintages, but with others, after about a year in oak, Hubert begins to make blends. When blending the brandy, many different lots may be combined and then the serious aging begins. Sometimes the final blending itself takes four to five years. It all depends on Hubert's taste and judgement. Aging is the criterion by which brandy and cognac are labeled. At Germain-Robin,

VSOP (very superior old pale) or Fine brandy has had a minimum of five years, and XO has had seven to eight years in the barrel.

In the dim light of the cellar, contemplating the amount of time it takes to create a finished brandy makes viewing the quiet beautiful barrels like standing before a shrine. The moment of reverence is quickly broken, however, when attention is drawn to the wall of barrels with the brass plaques on each. The plaques read like a list of Who's Who in California restaurants since Germain-Robin creates special blends for such luminaries as the Fog City Diner, Kuleto's, Mustards, the Lark Creek Inn, John Ash & Company, and Bix. Other businesses, such as Real Goods, Mendocino's emporium of biodynamic household goods, keep a barrel to bottle for gifts.

Consumer-sized barrels are the next topic of conversation. At the tasting table a sample ten-liter (one case) oak barrel is displayed. Keeping your own barrel filled with a favorite blend has the benefit of quicker aging. Two years in this small barrel is like twelve years in a big barrel. To illustrate the way the brandy changes color over the years, a series of seven test tubes are set up on a table in the distillery ranging from #1, the clear *eau-de-vie*, to #7, a rich deep-amber fifty-year-old sample.

When he isn't running the still, Hubert is often found in the laboratory adjacent to the cellar. Here he tastes samples of individual varietals at various stages. Their aromas and colors alone are so different, it becomes clearer to understand how Hubert is developing his complex brandies. The one from Semillon is like a finished non-floral brandy, with a short but fresh aroma. Chenin Blanc has the aroma of tropical fruits and a mellow creamy texture. An eight-year-old Pinot Noir transcends any previous experience of fine brandy when you inhale its deep fruit-rich aroma, and savor its caramel mid-flavor and long velvety finish. This is what all the waiting and attention to detail is about. There is no instant gratification in this business.

The story of how Hubert and Ansley met is a wonderous tale, as is the commitment to create a product that takes years to mature. The two men made that commitment and continue to make brandy without compromise. As Dan Berger queried in his column in the *Los Angeles Times*, "Is the world's best cognac made in Ukiah?"

MENDOCINO BREWING COMPANY

MENDOCINO BREWING COMPANY, HOPLAND BREWERY, BREWPUB, AND BEER GARDEN

13351 South Highway 101
P.O. Box 400
Hopland, CA 95449
Office: (707) 744-1015
Tavern: (707) 744-1361
Master brewer: Don Barkley
Brewery owners: Don Barkley, Norman Franks, Michael Laybourn, Michael Lovett, John Scahill

ACCESS

Location: Downtown Hopland on Highway 101.

Hours open for visits and tastings: 11:00 A.M.-9:00 P.M., Sunday-Friday; 11:00 A.M.-8:00 P.M., Saturday. Closed Thanksgiving and Christmas Day.

Appointment necessary for tour? Yes. Wheelchairs accommodated? Yes.

TASTINGS

Charge for tasting? Yes. One taste for 75 cents; set of 4 $3.00.

Typical beers offered: Peregrine Pale Ale, Red Tail Ale, Blue Heron Pale Ale, Black Hawk Stout; plus seasonal beers such as Springtide Ale, Eye of the Hawk, Yuletide Porter, and Frolic Shipwreck Ale (ask about its history!).

Sales of beer-related items? Yes, gift shop with glasses, mugs, hats, clothing, and a collection of beer memorabilia to view.

PROGRAMS

Special events? Music to dance to every weekend; 4th of July party; Anniversary party second Saturday in August; Octoberfest first weekend of October; St Patrick's Day Party in March. Beer garden available for parties.

THE RENAISSANCE OF MICRO-BREWING HIT HARD IN Mendocino County, where three breweries make some of the finest European-style beers in America. All have restaurants, tasting bars, and tours, and all are growing at phenomenal rates. They are each unique in many ways, besides the tastes of their beers. In 1983, the Mendocino Brewing Company became the first in California to open a brewpub since Prohibition. The Anderson Valley Brewing Company, on the site of Anderson Valley's oldest bar, names its beers with words from a bygone lingo. The North Coast Brewing Company, which has a pub in an old mortuary, is breaking records with its medal winners.

Here is a glimpse at what you'll find on the tour at each.

MENDOCINO BREWING COMPANY

The Mendocino Brewing Company is appropriately located in the town of Hopland, whose name indicates both a former era of glory as well as a contemporary success story. Named for the acres of hops that used to grow around the town, Hopland supplied tons of the flavorful dried cones of hop flowers to the first breweries in California. Now grapes have replaced hops; the hops for Mendocino's beers come from other areas of California and several western states. A hundred years ago, the part of the brick building that houses the bar was known as the Hop Vine Saloon. Now it is the Hopland Brewery, Brewpub, and Beer Garden. The north wall is still covered with the original stamped tin with a hop motif. A lively crowd populates the place from open to close for lunch, dinner, and weekend nights of live music.

Four beers—the signature Red Tail Ale, Peregrine Pale Ale, Blue Heron Pale Ale, and Black Hawk Stout—are always on tap. Seasonal brews, such as the spiced Springtide Ale, debut throughout the year. Samplers of the various beers are available. Sometimes the same beer is available from both a chilled keg and at room temperature (the British tradition known as cask-conditioned). Try a taste of each to compare flavors and see which one has the smoother mouth feel.

The Mendocino Brewing Company was started by five partners right after the California legislature legalized brewpubs in 1982. Two of the partners, Don Barkley and Michael Lovett, brought equipment and brewing skills from the New Albion Brewery in Sonoma, which closed in 1983. Their success (40- to 50-percent growth every year) pushed demand above the capabilities of the small brewery in Hopland, and in 1996, a new brewing facility was constructed ten miles north, right off Highway 101 in Ukiah. Tours can be taken of either the new brewery or of the original one in the back of the pub.

To take a tour of the original brewery, you meet the guide—usually one of the principals such as the brew master or the marketing director—at the bar, where a beer is immediately offered. Starting out with a taste helps you understand the processes which put the flavor in beer. Some of the highlights of the tour include seeing and smelling the malted barley in the mash tun (a stainless vessel) being steeped much like cream of wheat. Barley that is raised for beer is sold to professional malters, who kiln-dry the grain to make malted barley. Malt comes in different roasts. One, crystal, is like caramel and gives a red hue to beer. Another called "black patent," because of its espresso-like burn, contributes to a dry-style stout.

From the mash tun, the liquid, drawn from the malt and known as "sweet wort," flows via gravity into the next kettle, where it boils for one and a half hours with the hop flowers. The goal is to balance the sweetness of the malt with the bitterness imparted by the hops. Being able to smell the components at this stage helps to begin to understand the complex flavors in these beers. A glimpse in the refrigerated walk-in reveals 150-pound bales of hops. Inhaling their fragrance gives another aroma of the ultimate product.

A walk through the fermentation room passes two rows of eighty-barrel (2,480-gallon) stainless steel tanks, where the beer spends about two weeks. Next we see the bottling line. This brewery runs twenty-four hours a day, seven days a week, which keeps the conveyors and labeling machines in constant use. After bottling, the beer is kept for two weeks for "bottle conditioning," and the ultimate natural carbonation to take place. The cases of beer stacked ready for shipment are the last sight on the tour before returning to the bar.

ANDERSON VALLEY BREWING COMPANY

ANDERSON VALLEY BREWING COMPANY

Buckhorn Saloon
14081 Highway 128
P.O. Box 505
Boonville, CA 95415
(800) 207-BEER (2337)
fax (707) 895-2353

Master brewer: Ken Allen
Head brewer: Dave Towne
Brewery owners: Ken and
Kimberly Allen

ACCESS

Location: From Highway 101, take
Highway 128 west for about 26 miles
to Boonville; on north-east side of
the highway.

Hours open for visits and tastings:
Pub: 11:00 A.M.-9:00 P.M. daily,
June-September. Closed Wednesday,
April-May; closed Tuesday and
Wednesday, October-March. Closed
Thanksgiving and Christmas Day.

Appointment necessary for tour?
Generally yes, but may also happen
"by the moment."

Wheelchairs accommodated? Yes.

TASTINGS

Charge for tasting? Yes, $4.25 for 4
beers; $1.00-1.25 each additional
sample.

Typical beers offered: Boont Amber
ale, Poleeko Gold pale ale, Barney
Flats oatmeal stout, High Rollers
Wheat Beer, Belk's Extra Special Bitter
Ale, and Deepender's Dark porter;
plus seasonals such as India Pale Ale,
Raspberry Wheat Beer, October Fest,
Winter Solstice, Millennial, Cream
Port, and Whamber.

Sales of beer-related items? Yes, including mugs, hats, books, and clothing.

PROGRAMS

Special events? Newsletter; music
some nights in pub.

AS A STOP ON THE WAY TO OR FROM THE MENDOCINO COAST, or as a destination itself, the Anderson Valley Brewing Company has appeal. After pulling up in front of the Buckhorn Saloon in the middle of downtown Boonville, climb the stairs of the rough stained building, which was added on to the original saloon, dating from 1873. Mosey down and have a seat at the bar on one of the brass tractor seat stools.

Before or after a tour the way to sample the beers with the Boontling names is with the four-beer taster. Boontling is the language invented by the locals between 1880 and 1920, mainly to exclude outsiders. In 1987, when Ken and Kimberly Allen established the brewpub, they made the decision to pre-serve a few of Boontling's colorful words when naming their beers. That's why the wheat beer is known as High Rollers, a term once applied to the Yorkville area because of its high rolling hills. Light ale is Poleeko Gold (Poleeko refers to Philo), extra special ale is Boont Amber (Boont is Boonville), and an oatmeal stout is Barney Flats. While Barney Flats is Boontling for the area around Hendy Woods on the Navarro River, *barney* by itself means to embrace or kiss; plural it refers to cowboy boots. Take your pick. There are more references to Boontling in the menus and Brewery literature, as well as on signs around town. If this is your first exposure to Boontling, you might want to get a copy of the *Dictionary of Boontling* by Charles C. Adams. A few old-timers still speak it, but you probably won't hear them.

The original brewery is down the stairs under the pub's dining room. When demand challenged production, the decision was made to build a bigger facility. The new brewery is located at the south end of town just past the junction of Highway 253 which cuts over to Ukiah. Either one is available for touring. For tasting, you'll have to stay at the saloon; later you can go out in back and try your hand at horseshoes. Or you can stay inside and have *bahl gorms* (good food) at the pub.

NORTH COAST
BREWING COMPANY

444 North Main Street
Fort Bragg, CA 95437
(707) 964-3400
fax (707) 964-8768
Brewmaster: Mark Ruedrich
Brewery owners: Tom Allen, Joe
Rosenthal, Mark Ruedrich, et al.

ACCESS

Location: On Highway 1, also known as Main Street, in downtown Fort Bragg on the west side of the road.

Hours open for visits and tastings: 11:00 A.M.-5:30 P.M. daily, July-October; closed Sunday and Monday, November-June. Restaurant open same days until 9:00 P.M. Closed Thanksgiving Day, Christmas Day, New Year's Day.

Appointment necessary for tour? Tours offered 3:30 P.M. Tuesday-Friday; 1:30 P.M. Saturday. Reservations advised.

Wheelchairs accommodated? Yes.

TASTINGS

Charge for tasting? Yes, $3.50 for 4 beers, $7.00 for 8.

Typical beers offered: Blue Star Wheat Beer, Scrimshaw pilsner, Red Seal Ale, Old No. 38 Stout, Traditional Bock malt liquor, Old Rasputin Russian Imperial Stout, Christmas Ale.

Sales of beer-related items? Yes, including clothing, hats, books, and more.

PROGRAMS

Special events? Whale Watch Festival third weekend in March; brewmaster dinners (call for schedule); music in pub on weekend nights; mail order clothing, coasters, belt buckle, and magnets.

ON THE MENDOCINO COAST in Fort Bragg, the North Coast Brewing Company approaches micro-brewing with a cosmopolitan flair. Maybe it's because the brewmaster, Mark Ruedrich, apprenticed in England or because partner Tom Allen, who loves to visit Europe, came to the coast from a national advertising background. The third partner is building contractor Joe Rosenthal. When they opened the brewpub in 1988, the partners gave the food in the restaurant as much emphasis as the beer, of which Ruedrich's Red Seal Ale is the flagship.

Taking cues from the wine industry, the North Coast Brewing Company hosts Brewmaster dinners to showcase their beers' complexity and appropriateness with food. At

the dinners, besides educating your palate to the way malt, yeast, and hop-filled flavors go with barbecued venison osso bucco, linguine with smoked mushrooms, and pizza with rock shrimp, pancetta, brie, and chives, Mark leads you through the beer-making process. He also hands out a sheet of descriptors commonly used to describe the sweetness or toastiness of malt, the perfume and herbs of hops, and the vanilla or estery components of yeast.

The restaurant was once the original brewery, and it is still used for making small lots in the beautiful copper-clad brew kettle you see as soon as you walk in. Across the street from the restaurant, North Coast's fifteen thousand barrels of beer are brewed in a new facility that opened in 1994. Tours are offered every day at scheduled hours, but you are requested to call for a reservation due to the limited space on each. You will be taken from the eighty-thousand-pound grain silo step-by-step through the brewery to see the meticulous hands-on techniques required to make these premium beers. The critical degrees of timing and temperature are emphasized, as is the importance of testing and tasting for quality and consistency at all stages.

If you run into Mark, be sure to ask him about being a brewmaster. His passion for the art is immediately sensed in the intense sparkle of his eyes as he describes carefully selecting the hops and malt for each of his seven beers. Once, when questioned about making the final addition of hops—which imparts the most noticeable aroma to the finished beer— he couldn't resist the food connection. "It's like adding basil in the final minutes of cooking a tomato sauce."

THE APPLE FARM

THE APPLE FARM,
BATES & SCHMITT,
THE APPLE FARMERS

18501 Greenwood Road
Philo, CA 95466
(707) 895-2333; (707) 895-2461
Owners: Sally and Don Schmitt,
Karen and Tim Bates

ACCESS

Location: From Highway 101, take
Highway 128 west; continue about 35
miles to the Greenwood Ridge-Philo
Road and turn left. The driveway is
about 1/4 mile, just before the
bridge.

Hours: Daylight hours.

Appointment necessary for tour? Yes.

AMENITIES

Products: 60 varieties of fresh apples;
pomegranate jelly, plum jam, apricot
jam, raspberry jam, orange marmalade, apricot chutney, prune-plum
chutney, pear chutney, fig walnut
chutney, apple cider syrup, dried
apple wreaths, applewood chips,
apple twigs.

Events: Cooking classes offered by
single sessions, farm weekends, and
three days midweek; flower arranging
classes; Apple Day educational event
and lunch.

DYLLIC IS THE APPROPRIATELY WISTFUL SIGH AFTER A VISIT TO The Apple Farm. You might stop here on your way through Anderson Valley to buy apples, chutney, a dried apple wreath, or a bundle of orchard prunings for the barbecue. You might be coming to a cooking class. Or you may have made an appointment for a tour. One thing is sure, the energy and style of this family-run enterprise leaves a favorable impression.

On the outside, The Apple Farm isn't fancy. It is a working thirty-acre farm next to the Navarro River and across from Hendy Woods, one of California's most beautiful state parks. While the setting is lovely, the details done with flair, and the kitchen a dream-come-true, all of it is the result of a lot of hard work.

As soon as you get out of the car, you feel warmly embraced by the Schmitt and Bates families. Sally and Don Schmitt are in their "retirement" phase, after sixteen years as owners and chefs of the widely acclaimed French Laundry restaurant in Napa Valley. They purchased this property in 1983, and daughter and son-in-law, Karen and Tim Bates, moved in with their children. The Bates' background as gardeners was soon expanded as they learned all they could about the care and raising of apples, some of which have grown here for nearly a hundred years.

Almost any time you visit, mother and daughter are found in the kitchen across from the shed where the produce is dis-

played for sale. In 1995, the kitchen was remodeled to exude the feeling of Tuscany or Provence, or somewhere on the sunny Mediterranean where there is a lot of light. Creamy saffron walls with mint-green accents, diagonal oak floors, and hand-painted tiles on the hood and around the commercial range create the kind of work space you never want to leave. The attention to detail, such as a bouquet of asparagus on the counter, is repeated in other facets of the farm.

One sunny February day, I stopped by to tour and found Sally and Karen cutting Seville orange rinds for their marmalade. Don was putting the finishing touches on the greenhouse, and Tim was repairing the horse stable. Exemplifying the multi-generational focus in the kitchen, five-year-old Rita was on a stool with her own knife and pile of orange rinds, meticulously cutting them into equal pieces. Orange rinds aren't the only things cut by hand here. All the ingredients for the chutneys, too, are hand cut. Sally has never had a food processor, even when she had the restaurant. She says, "I don't know any better way to do this." One of the selling points of their products, she feels, is the identifiable pieces of nuts, lemon peels, cherries, and dates. In a reference to making their conserves in small batches, Sally relates that her mother always said never to work with more than four cups of fruit at a time. She and Karen stretch it to eight to ten cups, mostly determined by the size of their copper confiture pot.

In May, they are putting up the early raspberries. The apricots come in June, and then there's no stopping as the harvest of the garden and orchards goes into full swing. One of their most popular products is apple sauce made from the little pink pearl apples, most of which is sold at the Ferry Plaza Farmer's Market on Saturday mornings in San Francisco. Another is their apple cider syrup, a concentrated tart sauce for use in everything from meat marinades and stir-fries to ice cream toppings.

The tour of the rest of the farm reinforces what already appears to be a scene out of the good life. After a stop at the vegetable garden, we pass an old cabin left over from when the property was a family camp called River Rest. It is now the wood-fired apple drying shed. One of the innovative products Karen came up with is wreaths made from dried Jonathan and

Rome apples. In one three-year span they made eleven thousand of these edible and decorative wreaths for Smith & Hawken.

As we take a circular route around one part of the orchard, Karen shares her expertise on the varieties of apples they are growing, all of them organically. While most of the apples are still the original Red and Golden Delicious varieties, more interesting and antique varieties are being grafted over them. Rhode Island Green, Black Twig, Duchess of Oldenberg, Lady, and Lodi are the names of some of their sixty varieties. Another, Winter Banana, is pale yellow with a pink blush; it is typically used as a pollinator, but people love it for its strong fragrance. Some apples are great for eating, others are better for cooking. The Apple Farm's juice is pressed from Greening, Sierra Beauty, and Pippins. When Karen and Tim first started, they sold their apples to the cannery, but over the years they have created their own market.

Now, once a week they load the truck and take boxes of hard-to-find varieties to markets in the Bay Area.

Visitors to the farm will find lugs and bags of fresh apples, plus juice and The Apple Farm chutneys and preserves, stocked in a produce stand next to the barn. Karen cuts a few apples so customers can sample the differences. A chalkboard above lists the available produce and prices. She hosts an Apple Day at the farm in the fall. The Apple Farm also provides one of the big booths at the Mendocino County Fair and Apple Show in September. At both, tastes and educational information are shared.

More visitors pull up, and I watch their expressions as they walk around and take deep breaths of the sweet air. As they survey the pastoral surroundings, smiles indicate their first impression. But they have all the rest of The Apple Farm to experience. When they leave, I think I know what they'll sigh.

CAFE BEAUJOLAIS BAKERY AND BRICKERY

961 Ukiah Street
Mendocino, CA 95460
(800) 930-0443; (707) 937-0443;
restaurant (707) 937-5614

Owners: Margaret Fox and
Christopher Kump

ACCESS

Location: From Highway 1, turn west at the stop light on Little Lake Street; turn left on School Street (the first left) and continue 2 blocks to Ukiah Street. It is in front of you.

Appointment necessary for tour? Yes, for Brickery and Garden.

Hours: Brickery by appointment. Restaurant hours: 5:45 P.M.-9:00 P.M. nightly. Closed Thanksgiving. Variable winter closures.

AMENITIES

Products: Brick-oven baked breads: Mendocino Sourdough, sourdough baguettes, Red Seal Rye, Austrian Seed Loaf, olive rosemary foccacia, buckwheat hazelnut, potato walnut, panini al cioccolata, pizza dough and pillows, rye currant.

Mail order catalog: Panforte, Dried Fruitcakes, Chocolate-Covered Graham Crackers, Spicy Gingersnaps, English Toffee, Buttercream Caramels, Fuller's Fine Herb Blends and Herb Vinegars; Nut Crunch Nut Butter; pear barbecue sauce; Navarro Vineyards Verjus; Woofer's Fabulous Dog Biscuit Mix; Austrian Seed Breakfast food; cashew granola; waffle & pancake mix; hot chocolate mix; Austrian Seed Bread loaves.

Events: Full restaurant; garden tours by appointment May-August, call (707) 937-1856 for reservations.

CAFE BEAUJOLAIS IS THE BUSINESS THAT PUT MENDOCINO ON the nation's culinary map. For years, Margaret Fox's breakfasts were synonymous with Mendocino. Then Christopher Kump came along and applied his considerable talents to dinners. In the meantime, he and Fox married, and the Cafe Beaujolais Bakery, mail order, and Brickery have expanded the legend.

When Margaret Fox bought Cafe Beaujolais in 1977, she couldn't have anticipated the acclaim she and her little restaurant would receive over the decades. Such culinary noteworthies as Julia Child, Marcella Hazan, and Diana Kennedy have joined thousands of tourists and food groupies who come to Mendocino specifically to eat at the "Beauj," as we locals affectionately call one of California's "in" places to dine.

Fox, herself, is celebrated as one of America's top women chefs. When she isn't tending the stove in her own kitchen, she often does guest appearances for culinary benefits in Napa Valley, San Francisco, and New York. She also contributes mightily to the homefront where she is spearheading a major fundraising effort for a cancer research and information center on the coast. Kump, a professionally trained chef, has contributed work on behalf of the Certified Organic movement and the establishment of the Farmer's Market, an event in town every Friday from May through October.

Although she grew up in a home with a "million cookbooks" and with a mother who "is a marvelous cook," Fox didn't start out to be a professional cook. Her degree from the University of California at Santa Cruz is in developmental psychology. She came to Mendocino to look around and inquire about work, and within a day she had a job as a baker at the Mendocino Hotel. From there she apprenticed at a couple of other places before plunging into restaurant ownership.

Fox is a self-taught cook with an inquisitive nature. At the Beaujolais, she initially specialized in her favorite meal of the day, breakfast. Not content with breakfast mastery, Fox combined her innate business sense with her culinary talent to maximize the potential of the restaurant. She established a mail order bakery business so fans could get a taste of the Cafe Beaujolais when they couldn't actually be here. In 1983 she

sent out her first catalog featuring panforte, the chewy Italian fruit and nut cake acclaimed by critics to be better than most in Italy. Since then she's added Dried-Fruit Fruitcakes, Chocolate-Covered Graham Crackers, Spicy Gingersnaps, raspberry and blackberry jams, and pear barbecue sauce from pears grown in an orchard behind her home.

After the success of two cookbooks, *Cafe Beaujolais Cookbook* and *Morning Food*, co-authored with John Bear, Fox added waffle and pancake mix, cashew granola, and hot chocolate mix to the catalog to appease breakfast lovers who missed her specialties. Taking cues from her black labrador retrievers, she has recently included a couple of varieties of dog biscuit mixes. Bread by mail has also become a reality. Austrian seed bread is baked in the wood-fired brick oven Fox and Kump built in 1989. These meal-in-a-loaf moist round loaves are shipped three times a week.

The wood-fired oven is housed in its own building, known as the Brickery, in the Cafe Beaujolais Garden. While tours of the garden are scheduled at various times, my recommendation for getting a sense of Cafe Beaujolais is to see how bread is baked on the stone hearth. Since I happen to live across the street, nothing makes me hungrier than the fresh, yeasty aromas that blow through my windows on a south wind. Even when the wind is from the north, I check periodically in the morning for reassuring signs of the smoke and steam that billow up the Brickery's chimney.

The baker gives tours by appointment. Be prepared to get up early because that's what bakers do. He comes in at five o'clock to start the fire; to see the most action, eight is perfect. By then, five cubic feet of oak and madrone have burnt down to very hot embers and heated the brick oven to about 600 degrees. All six or seven loads are baked in heat retained from the hot fire. The Cafe Beaujolais logo bird is carved on the handcrafted oven door. Although it resembles an antique woodcut that must surely have a story, it was designed on a whim by the late Stephanie Kroninger, a graphic artist of local renown.

French and American bread posters decorate the white walls of the Brickery's functional space, which houses mixers,

ingredients, and a proofing closet filled with rising loaves. While the oven heats, sourdough baguettes are shaped and arranged on metal pans perforated with tiny holes and set to rise. They are first to go in the oven. As soon as they are in place, water is sprayed on them and the door is closed. That blast of steam, which I count on seeing from my window much as I look for whale spouts in the ocean, creates wonderful crunchy crusts.

Each successive bake drops the oven temperature about 150 degrees. After the baguettes go the rounds of sourdough, which have risen in floured *bannetons*, French rising baskets. Three loaves at a time are dumped from the baskets onto a wooden peel, a long-handled flat paddle. Their tops are floured and sliced in a signature design, and they are slid off the peel onto the oven floor. Slicing the top of a loaf of bread before it goes into the oven is necessary for even rising because once the dough hits that heat it has an initial spring and pouf. By that time, the crust has also set from the

heat, and any other rising that might come from the inside can happen more evenly if small cuts are made in the dough. Once the baguettes come out of the oven, a sample is irresistible. With the kind of crust that only comes from a brick oven, such a moist crumb, and just minutes from the oven—this is the way bread is meant to be eaten.

As the oven cools, the morning bake continues with lighter, yeasted breads. Next is the Red Seal Rye, which intensifies the yeastiness in the air with its dose of North Coast Brewery's beer. Then come the dense loaves of Austrian Seed Bread.

On many days, the top of the Brickery's Dutch door to the garden is open, and you can stop by to say hello. Upstairs, the bread is sold at a take-out window at the restaurant; it is also distributed to a few of the coast's markets. In addition to buying the bread and dining at the restaurant, you can pick up a mail order catalog. It's the Cafe Beaujolais way to bring home a taste of Mendocino.

NOYO HARBOR
Fort Bragg, CA 95437
Noyo Harbor District information
(707) 964-4719
CAITO FISHERIES
19400 South Harbor Drive
Fort Bragg, CA 95437
(707) 964-6368
ACCESS
Location: North side for restaurants, retail outlets, and party boats: Turn east on North Harbor Drive on the north side of the Noyo Bridge and follow it down to the fishing port and access to the mouth of the river. South side for Noyo Harbor District & Caito Fisheries: From Highway 1, turn east on Highway 20 and take South Harbor Drive. To get to Caito, bear to the left just past Thanksgiving Coffee and turn onto the one lane road. Park and walk to the building. To get to the harbor, follow the road to the right.
Appointment necessary for tour? Yes, for Caito Fisheries and Party Boats. Self-guided tours around Noyo Harbor.
AMENITIES
Special events or programs? The annual Salmon Barbecue held on the Fourth of July Weekend is a Noyo Women for Fisheries benefit for salmon hatcheries. Phone (707) 961-6300 for tickets and information.
Eureka Fisheries Fish and Chips and Market, 32410 North Harbor Drive. Open daily 11:00 A.M.-6:00 P.M. (707) 964-1600.
Party Boats: (Need fishing license if over 16. One-day licenses available at boats for $5.75.)
Lady Irma II, P.O. Box 103, Fort Bragg, CA 95437. (707) 964-3854. 5-hour trips at 7:00 A.M. and 1:00 P.M. $45.00 includes rod and reel and bait, $40.00 if bringing own rod and reel.

NOYO HARBOR EXUDES THE CHARM OF A WORKING EUROPEAN fishing village, perhaps one on the Amalfi peninsula south of Naples, or on the Sicilian coast east of Palermo. Italian names such as Palladini, Alioto, Lazio, Cavellini, and Caito dominated the local fishing industry here from its inception in the 1880s until its heyday in the 1970s. As you cross the bridge, high over the mouth of Noyo River, the view to the west of the breakwater harbor entrance often includes a fishing boat motoring in, its hard-earned catch in the hold, its crab pots on the deck. On the east side of the bridge, where the river makes an s-turn, the banks are built up with restaurants and the remnants of fish processing plants. Where there were once nearly a dozen plants, there are now three or four.

Caito Fisheries, which started out on the north side in the 1920s and moved across the river in the 1930s, is the oldest fish processor in Noyo. Now owned by its fourth generation, Caito processes millions of pounds of local crab, cod, sole, snapper, rock fish and salmon every year. Great-grandfather John Baptist Caito, the son of a fisherman, immigrated to the United States from Sicily in 1885. His story parallels that of other Italian families in California's fishing industry. After making his way across the United States, he joined his cousins, named Lazio, in San Francisco. At first he concentrated on salmon in the Sacramento River, processed them in Pittsburg, and started the Western Fish Company. After the earthquake decimated production facilities in 1906, many fishing people joined together to form new companies. Caito's venture became the California Western Fish Company, and by the early 1920s he had established processing plants in Santa Barbara and Eureka, as well as at Noyo.

From the 1920s through the 1970s Noyo Harbor was a wild and bustling place. Baby Face Nelson, a notorious bandit, was a coast regular. One of the sales people at Caito Fisheries tells how his father used to catch abalone that Baby Face used for bait. The seclusion of Noyo Harbor and the way the docks were built made this a perfect place for bootlegging during Prohibition. A twelve-inch space between the timbers that held the docks and the dock platform was the right size for stashing bottles of booze until the fish were unloaded and accounted for by the authorities. Another method of bringing in the illegal hooch was to throw a case overboard and let it sink into the not-too-deep water. A stick tied to the case with a string floated to the surface so it could be retrieved at a safe time.

Noyo moves at a slower pace now than it did in the 1970s, when the fleet was at its peak and salmon season was a major event. When Joe Caito, the great-grandson of John, took over his family plant in 1975 and named it Caito Fisheries, Noyo was a still a vital and seasonal fishing enclave, but with the recent shutdown of salmon fishing, the local fleet has become decimated. Now fishing is primarily for the colorful array of bottom fish such as black cod and channel rock, a bright red-skinned fish. And of course crab. Instead of owning their own boats, fish houses like Caito now buy from privately-owned vessels. In addition to the Italians, other names which emblazoned fish houses included Cummings, Meredith, Schnaubelt, and Cal Shell. Today, Grader Fish House is a reincarnation of one of the early family names, and Eureka Fisheries has taken over one of the oldest buildings.

Dolphin Charters, 32450 North Harbor Drive, Fort Bragg, CA 95437. (707) 964-7441. 5-hour trips at 7:00 A.M. and 1:00 P.M. $55.00 includes rod and reel and bait.

Misty II Charters, P.O. Box 1104, Fort Bragg, CA 95437. (707) 964-7161. 5-hour trips at 7:00 A.M. and 1:00 P.M. $45.00 includes rod and reel and bait, $40.00 if bringing own rod and reel.

Patty-C Charter Fishing, P.O. Box 572, Fort Bragg, CA 95437. (707) 964-0669. 5-hour trips at 7:00 A.M. and 1:00 P.M. $55.00 includes rod & reel & bait.

Tally Ho Sport Fishing, P.O. Box 2509, Fort Bragg, CA 95437. (707) 964-2079. 5-hour trips at 7:00 A.M. and 1:00 P.M. $50.00 includes rod and reel and bait.

Sights of the past and a look at the present state of commercial fishing can be had by a self-guided walk around the harbor. All the restaurants serve the freshest seafood in the world from dining rooms overlooking the picturesque harbor. Eureka Fisheries has a retail outlet, as well as a kitchen from which to buy crisp, greaseless fish and chips. Eating them at picnic tables on the deck overlooking the river is a great way to take in the action, most of which centers around the gang of vociferous sea lions. They moved into the river about ten years ago and have proliferated. Their fat, lazy existence consists of entertaining the tourists and begging for food, which should not be given no matter how loud they bark.

While walking around the harbor, you can glimpse fish processing in action through open doors of processors. As boats dock, they unload their catch of bottom fish, crab, or sea urchins on a regular basis. The fish are cleaned and filleted or packed whole to be shipped around the country. From July through September, signs are posted giving the berth number of a boat from which you can buy the premium albacore tuna directly from a fisherman. The silvery fat fish are caught about a hundred miles offshore and flash-frozen at sea. Local residents make the pilgrimage to Noyo during albacore season to fillet and put up hundreds of pounds in canning jars. In winter months, crab comes in and is soon plunged into huge commercial pots of boiling water. You can tell it's sea urchin season when you see stacks of the purple spiked shells looking like a burial pile of petrified hedgehogs.

To catch your own fish, a number of party boats are moored in Noyo. Five hour trips are offered twice a day. For one price, all the tackle and equipment is provided, except a fishing license. One-day licenses can be purchased from the boats or the local fishing store. Bring your own food and warm clothing since the Pacific is chilly any time of the year. Equipped with expert fishing advice and insider's knowledge of the best sites, the boats are a rewarding way to try your own hand at continuing the fishing legacy endowed over the years by this charming harbor.

EAGLE ROCK GOURMET LAMB

SHEEP RAISING HAS BEEN A MAJOR INDUSTRY IN MENDOCINO County for 150 years, and today over sixteen thousand sheep and lambs are raised annually for meat and wool. Among the premier grazing spots are the rolling hills from Yorkville to Philo. Whether due to the tender native grasses, the moist cool mornings and warm sunny days, or the access to plenty of free-ranging exercise, lamb from this stretch of Anderson Valley tastes better than that from anywhere else.

"Gourmet Lamb Delivered Nationwide" reads the sign along Highway 128 near Yorkville. It also marks the home of Stanley Johnson, who owns and runs the Johnson Ranch. His most recent venture is selling frozen lamb by mail order but he comes from a long history of Mendocino sheep ranching.

The first of Johnson's kin came to Anderson Valley in 1859. They initially settled around Philo and then near Navarro, at the west end of the valley. They eventually moved to Glen Ellen in Sonoma County, where Stanley's father, Glen, was born. In 1919, Glen came to Mendocino County, where he bought the original 1,100 acres of this ranch. Now the holdings have grown to 2,250 acres. For some forty years, Glen's business was hauling. He hauled lambs from the Valley to market in his truck. Stanley's mother, Helen, was born in Laytonville in the north part of the county. Both parents passed away in the 1970s; and Stanley, who has had cerebral palsy since he was six weeks old, has been running the ranch from his wheelchair ever since. His two sisters married and live elsewhere.

"We always had sheep," says Stanley. These days he tries to keep about six hundred head, but that number fluctuates dramatically because of the mountain lion and coyote problem.

By calling ahead you can stop by the Johnson Ranch, have a close-up view of the sheep, and visit with Stanley while he describes the phases of raising lamb for market. While here, you can order some to take home or have it shipped.

Around the first of August, the ewes get pregnant; their 147-day gestation ends in January or February when most lambs are born. At this point farmers have to worry about weather as much as predators. One nearby farmer lost 63 per-

cent of her lambs one year because the storms were so bad many of the newborns drowned. As soon as they are born, they are brought into pens to have their tails docked. During the next few months, the sheep get herded up on the hills. This is when the predator problem is the worst. The mountain lions and coyotes always kill the biggest lambs first," says Johnson. One of his neighbors told me about going to a Woolgrowers Convention where the keynote speaker equated raising lambs with being a gambler. "Weather, crop, coyote, mountain lions—it's a gamble."

In May, the lambs weigh about eighty pounds. At this point there isn't much fat and the meat comes out to about forty pounds. They are brought back down from the hills and

trucked to the USDA approved butcher in Sonoma County. They are processed and flash frozen, which, according to Johnson, doesn't affect the flavor. For shipping, the meat is packed in dry ice and will stay frozen for three to seven days. You can buy a whole or half lamb, or the front or hind quarters. The meat is cut and wrapped in portions of roasts, chops, racks, legs, and shanks, each serving three or four. A brochure details all the cuts and prices.

To buy lamb at the ranch, calling ahead is a must. Otherwise, visitors are welcome to come by and meet Johnson, learn about the successes and pitfalls of being in the lamb business, and see the cared-for lambs up close. Taking into consideration what a gamble this business is, when the lambs are harvested you might wonder if it's worth it. Just put a chop or lamb rib from Anderson Valley on the grill some hot summer night. The quality of naturally raised lamb can't be beat. In case you can't decide how to prepare it, Stanley slips some recipes from the Anderson Valley Woolgrowers' *Bo-Peep Cookbook* in each order.

GOWAN'S OAK TREE FRUIT STAND

MENDOCINO APPLES HAVE BEEN EXPORTED TO MARKETS and canneries for more than a hundred years. The crop is so important that the county fair, held every September, is called the Mendocino County Fair and Apple Show. It may be the premier event in the world where you can see and sample scores of apple varieties from antiques to new hybrids.

Among the oldest apple-growing families in the county are the Gowans. They have been growing apples and other produce on their 265-acre ranch along Highway 128 in Anderson Valley since the 1880s. Jim and Josephine Gowan head the family business, which grows sixty varieties of apples, thirty-eight kinds of peaches, and a wide variety of apricots, berries, cherries, and prunes. They also plant twenty-five acres of vegetables.

Some of the apple trees on the property are over a hundred years old. That's when Jim's grandfather, George Studebaker, came west from Missouri by covered wagon. He traded horses for land and eventually ended up with the property near Philo. In the 1880s, he regularly loaded his wagon with apples and

made the three-day round trip to Mendocino to peddle them. His daughter Alice married Cecil Gowan, from an Irish family in Shelter Cove. In 1922, Cecil took over the business and expanded the produce distribution along the coast from Fort Bragg to Gualala. By the 1930s, Alice was selling boxes of apples under the namesake oak tree, and the roadside produce stand has been a fixture in Anderson Valley ever since.

The stand has an irresistible pull for travelers along Highway 128, myself included. Any time of the year, the open counters are piled with sacks of apples, cherries, zucchini, tomatoes, and fifty other fruits and vegetables. On a sweltering summer day, we always stop for an apple juice popsicle or an ice-cold glass of juice. In the winter, we pick up containers of apple juice to take home, plus whatever strikes our fancy from the day's harvest. Lugs of apples for canning are always stacked against the wall. A chalkboard overhead lists the produce in season and prices.

For people used to eating supermarket apples, which have been in cold storage since being picked, coming to Gowan's provides a revelation in flavors. The first apples of the season, around July 1, are Red Astrachan, good only for baking and canning and "making the best apple sauce." Then come apples with names like Yellow Transparent, Crimson Beauty, and Beacon. The beloved Gravensteins are in full harvest between August 1 and September 30. During that time, the King of Tompkin, a good eating and baking apple, and the all-purpose McIntosh also come into season. In fact, the McIntosh is picked well into November. If you remember an apple from your youth and you wonder if it is still available, it might just be grown here. Many antique varieties such as Sweetspice (in July), Orange Pippin (August), Spartan and Gloria Mundi (September), and Ida Red and Arkansas Black (October) are found here. Rome Beauty is the last apple to be picked, usually in November. One of Jim's favorites is Sweet Spice, an early apple which is "real sweet." This may be the only place it is raised any more. With so many varieties to keep track of, the Gowans have published a free booklet that details the uses and harvest time of their apples and all of the other fruits and vegetables in this veritable cornucopia.

Jim Gowan is always grafting and trying new varieties. When he leads a tour, he can point to any tree in the orchard and give its grafting history. With ninety trees planted on each of a hundred acres, that is amazing. Learning about grafting is my favorite part of the tour. Several varieties can be grafted on the same trunk, and new varieties usually are grafted onto a producing tree so it doesn't lose production while the graft takes. It takes three or four years for a graft to produce a usable amount of fruit, but a newly planted tree takes five to seven years to have apples.

While leading the tour through the orchard and packing plant, Jim describes a year in the life of a fruit orchard. Pruning is done in January and February. In March the trees begin to blossom. The trees are sprayed with imoden, an organic phosphate, at various times to control the moths that cause wormy apples. This is especially worrisome during the late rains, when the trees are budding and the leaves are coming out.

From April through July the apples are thinned. This is a very meticulous and challenging process, says Jim. In the bud stage, each little unwanted bud is rolled off by hand.

When the apples are as big as walnuts, it is even harder to get the job done well. Sometimes as much as 90 percent of the apples are cut off the trees. The reason for such severe thinning is that it reduces the potentially devastating load on the trees.

When harvest begins, everyone works six days a week. Apples for the fruit stand and produce markets are packed in forty-pound lugs. About 50 percent of the harvest goes to the cannery, so as soon as they are picked, all the apples are chilled down in cold storage. Next they move down conveyor belts, where they are washed and sorted. Apples shipped to produce markets out of the area are waxed, but not those for the roadside stand. "Here, everyone wants them just as they come off the trees," says Jim.

That's what you find at Gowan's. A heritage of apple farming and a whole lot more keep this family busy. Four of their seven children are living and working on the farm. And, in what feels like making a complete circle, Jim and Jo Gowan load up a truck twice a week and head to the farmers' markets in Fort Bragg and Mendocino, just like their relatives did over seventy years ago.

McFadden Farm

McFadden Farm

Potter Valley, CA 95469

(800) 343-5636; (707) 743-1122

Owner: Guinness McFadden

Access

Location: From Highway 101, take Highway 20 east to Potter Valley Road; follow it 2 miles to the first fork, turn left on West Road and go 3½ miles to the stop sign at Main Street. Go straight across Main 1¼ miles to Gibson, turn left, and continue 7-800 yards; turn right on Power House Road, continue to the end, and turn left into the farm.

Hours: By appointment.

Appointment necessary for tour? Yes.

Amenities:

Products: McFadden Farm dried herbs, herb blends, bay wreaths, garlic braids, sun-dried tomatoes, organic produce and grapes.

MCFADDEN FARM PRODUCTS ARE TILLED AND MARKETED from the exquisitely precious Potter Valley on the east side of Mendocino County. In this fruitful haven watered by the Russian River, Guinness McFadden produces an up-market assortment of herbs, grapes, garlic, and wild rice. A native New Yorker, Notre Dame graduate, and ex-naval officer with a stint at Stanford's business school, he is not your typical back-to-the-lander.

On the picturesque five-hundred-acre farm he bought in 1970, Guinness combines his business sense with a penchant for anticipating trends in the California food scene. He does it all with organically produced crops and is best known for the line of herbs with the distinctive California quail on the label. He packs the herbs in whole-leaf form, giving the cook the first chance at crushing the flavor from basil, tarragon, sage, or oregano. His line of herb blends races ahead of the competition by combining "chunks" of dried garlic and onions.

Arriving at the farm, I always feel this is someplace special, no matter which season it is. So much is growing, something is always being dried, packed, or tied together, scenting the air with herbaceous aromas. Guinness, a robust father of five with dark Irish eyebrows and a strong masculine voice, comes out of the gray office building/warehouse to greet me.

We head around the building to take a short tour. First stop is the vineyards. McFadden Farm has 140 acres, all organically grown, of Sauvignon Blanc, Chardonnay, Gewürztraminer, Johannisberg Riesling, and Zinfandel grapes that he sells to Fetzer and to other wineries such as Hanna in Sonoma and Beringer in Napa.

Next, we wind past the prolific vegetable garden, which is grown for the McFadden family and crew. Tomatoes, however, are another commercial crop. Five to six tons of dried tomatoes are processed a year. First they are halved and dried in the air and sun. When they reach the perfect stage, they are seasoned and packed in jars with organic olive oil.

Next to the road the north fork of the Russian River rushes through the property. On the other side, above the river, is Guinness's house, with its panoramic view of the farm and valley. A beautiful covered bridge, reminiscent of New England, crosses the river. Next to it is the power plant he built to generate electricity for the western side of Potter Valley. A dam with a sixteen-foot fall creates the force that operates the generating machine.

With all this water, it's understandable why Guinness chose to make his living growing a variety of crops. As we turn from the bridge we cross the road for a closer inspection of the herbs, in patches and by the acre. In March seeds for the annuals such as basil, tarragon, savory, and dill are sown in flats in the greenhouse. The bulk of McFadden Farm's thirty acres of herbs are annuals. There is an acre of rosemary, a perennial, which, when pruned, is cut very low so it doesn't get woody, and three quarters of an acre of marjoram. Lavender, the characteristic flavor in herbes de Provence, is another perennial. In the summer its silvery base is rife with aromatic purple tassles; in winter the low-cut clumps look like rows of wide-wale corduroy. Guinness attributes the climate in Potter Valley as exceptional for growing herbs and contributing to their especially high oil content and flavor. He has also developed a market for the woody part of basil after the leaves have been harvested. The stalks are left until the first freeze, then they are cut, dried, and packed to throw on a barbecue fire as aromatics.

Each year, Guinness and his crew process over 170,000 pounds of garlic. Visitors from August until well into September will find a crew in the field under a canopy braiding the perfect bulbs into long strands for Williams-Sonoma and other specialty stores. While not rivaling Gilroy in the release of pungency in the air, the piles of garlic everywhere are a sight to behold, as is the beauty of the finished products.

In addition to the grapes, herbs, and garlic, there are hedgerows of raspberries and thickets of wild blackberries; the berries of both are made into jam. McFadden Farm is also one of the pioneers of wild rice cultivation in California. The nutty-tasting black kernels, known as the caviar of grains, are not really rice at all but come from an aquatic grass native to Minnesota.

Behind Guinness's office is the mill, a work in progress for processing herbs, which are harvested from July through

August. Milling involves a crew of sorters, a machine that separates the leaves by size between screens, and a vibrating table to remove debris. The perfect herb leaves go to one side and the debris to the other. A separate room is reserved for packing the herbs into jars and combining the blends such as Mexican, Seafood, Salad, Lamb, Grill, and Herbes de Provence. From September well into March, bay laurel leaves from the farm and from Yorkville, on the other side of the county, are made into wreaths. Skilled workers tie and fill in the forms amidst a heady aroma that hangs in the air.

When you visit the farm, there may be other activities going on. With three kids still at home, someone is always coming and going, or fishing, horseback riding, or doing chores. This is a special place to grow up, and even more special because the McFaddens are sharing so much of the bounty in such useful and creative ways.

MENDOCINO BOUNTY
SPECIALTY MARKETPLACE
200 South School Street
Ukiah, CA 95482
(707) 463-6711
Owner: Karen Record

ACCESS

Location: Downtown Ukiah; from Highway 101, take the Perkins Street offramp; turn west and follow it to School Street, turn left; the shop is on the right.

Hours: 9:30 A.M.-5:30 P.M. Monday-Saturday, 9:30 A.M.-8:00 P.M daily in December; Closed Easter Sunday, July 4th, Thanksgiving, Christmas Day, New Year's Day.

AMENITIES

Products: Complete line of Mendocino condiments, preserves, and wines.

Events: Mendocino Bounty at Fetzer Vineyards in August. Call for in-store schedule.

HOT PEPPER JELLY COMPANY
330 North Main Street
Fort Bragg, CA 95437
(800) 892-4823; (707) 961-1422
fax (707) 964-5462
Owner: Carol Hall

ACCESS

Location: Downtown Fort Bragg, on the east side of Main Street (Highway 1).

Hours: 10:00 A.M.-5:30 P.M. Monday-Saturday; 10:30 A.M.-5:00 P.M. Sunday. Closed Easter Sunday, Thanksgiving, Christmas Day, New Year's Day.

AMENITIES

Products: Complete line of Hot Pepper Jelly Company and Mendocino-made condiments and preserves. Mail order catalog.

WHILE THE FERTILE SOIL AND RELATIVELY UNSPOILED OCEAN have been sources of Mendocino's daily sustenance for as long as people have settled here, within the past two decades an influx of industrious newcomers, drawn by the land, the sea, and the communities, has added another dimension to making a living off the land.

This feisty bunch of entrepreneurs is an energetic mix of farmers, teachers, ex-hippies, back-to-the-landers, and business school graduates. They are self-starters who hustle to compete in urban outlets in order to maintain their rural lifestyle. Those with the longest or most unique histories are profiled in their own sections. Here I want to introduce a few more of the cottage industries and their products. The businesses are too small to accommodate visitors for tours, but outlets throughout the county, as well as mail-order sources, feature their foods. An extensive listing is in the Resources section.

One of the biggest success stories in the county is The Cheesecake Lady, founded in 1982 by Robin Collier and her cousin, Paul Leviton. Located on the main street in Hopland, they sell a million slices of cheesecake every year. With fourteen slices to each cheesecake, that means seventy-five thousand cheesecakes are made and shipped all over the world.

Carol Hall, a native of Louisiana, moved to the Mendocino coast in 1971. She came with her retired chemist husband to live off the land and soon began marketing an organic compost known as Albert's Best. Coming from the Creole tradition where cooking is a big part of life, Hall focused her own first commercial culinary endeavors on her heritage. She developed her line of hot pepper jellies in 1985, while cooking in a restaurant. Since then, she opened her shop on Main Street and developed a long line of condiments, both sweet and savory. She also has a mail-order catalog that features a premier selection of Mendocino-made jams, jellies, salad dressings, preserves, and mustards.

Someone who has made Mendocino and mustard synonymous is Devora Rossman. In 1977, while teaching preschool, Rossman got into mustard making. She started out mixing the first batches on a table in a converted chicken coop. Now she makes and distributes 15,000 cases a year from a 1,550-square-foot warehouse north of Fort Bragg. Visiting her space, with its view of the ocean from the sliding shipping doors, shows what a hands-on process making Mendocino Mustard continues to be. Four to six employees combine the ingredients batch by batch and fill, label, and box the jars for orders shipped from coast to coast. In addition to her addictive sweet-hot original recipe, a new product, Seeds & Suds, has joined the line. This one includes whole mustard seeds and a dose of Red Seal Ale from the North Coast Brewery down the street.

With Mendocino Mustard leading the way, other local mustard makers followed. The Little River Inn produces whole seed and garlic-flavored mustards. Lionel and Rose Jacob make an extensive line of twelve mustards and several salad dressings under the Noyo Reserve label. Some of the innovative mustard combinations made by these Fort Bragg residents are garlic Dijon, red pepper, orange espresso, and—yes—chocolate fudge mustard.

Herbs and vinegar are made by several cottage producers. Fuller's Fine Herbs are produced in Little River. Arlene Fuller, who has a degree in food science and moved to the coast from the Haight-Ashbury district in San Francisco in the early 1970s, raises basil, oregano, dill, sage, and tarragon on a slope behind her cozy farmhouse. Fuller's herbs are carefully dried and packed singly or in blends. In addition, Arlene flavors white wine vinegar, composing such blends as lemon-garlic,

dill parsley, and my favorite, Winter Thyme, which includes sprigs of thyme and whole cranberries.

Good Thyme Herb Company is the name of Debra Dawson's enterprise in Caspar, a tiny town between Mendocino and Fort Bragg. Debra names her herb blends for specific uses or for the story of their creation, all of which can be read about in her *Good Thyme Herb Blends Cookbook*.

Oscar Stedman, a self-taught cook who came to the coast in 1979, makes a line of salad dressings that includes her popular garlic basil dressing. On the east side of Mendocino County, dressings are made by Tobina's Specialty Foods in Ukiah and Juliana's Cafe in Willits.

Chutneys are another popular condiment, and Mendocino provides some of the best. Carol Hall makes apple apricot, mango pear, and cranberry orange chutneys. Debbie Drummond, of Mendocino, produces a line of Drummond Farms Fresh Fruit Chutneys, featuring ginger pear, apple currant, and raspberry. More fruit-based chutneys and excellent jams are made by Mendocino Jams and Preserves. They are beautifully packaged and sold at a country-style store front on Main Street in Mendocino.

Also in the cottage line of producers is Laurie Ackerman. She started out making moist chocolate chip and lemon bundt cakes in Fort Bragg in 1992. Distinctively packaged in brightly colored cellophane, these cakes have found a big niche for consumers nationwide. Ackerman sells ten thousand retail and mail-order cakes every year.

The wildest tastes of Mendocino come from the coastal side of the county. From the ocean shores and the forest floor come sea vegetables and mushrooms, two products that have been successfully marketed because of the ingenuity of a few people and the subsequent demand of appreciative consumers.

The common seaweed we see bobbing in the tidal waters or being slung around by children on the beach has been elevated to an important ingredient due the increasing awareness of a health-conscious public. The slinky green kelp is loaded with nutrients and has numerous gourmet and healing uses, such as helping to reduce stress and to eliminate radioactive poisons from the body. John and Eleanor Lewellan, of the Mendocino Sea Vegetable Company, came to the coast from the Bay Area in search of a more peaceful organic lifestyle. They found northern California to be one of the richest habitats for edible seaweeds in the world, and since 1980, they have been harvesting and drying ten varieties of seaweed and marketing them throughout the United States. The clean ocean water along Mendocino's coast makes it an especially good source. "We have a responsibility to maintain and champion the relatively pristine ocean that provides us with such nutritious food," says Eleanor. She is one of the leaders in the fight against offshore oil development, an issue that has about 99.9% support among residents.

Another sea vegetable product is made from the bullwhip kelp that litters the beaches. Pickles From the Sea, made by Jerry Westfall in Mendocino, are jars of sliced kelp marinated in dill and other flavored vinegars. Crisp and tasty, while novel, they are also quite delicious.

With sea vegetables at the base of the ecological system, mushrooms are a step up. After the first rains and well into spring, you'll see signs saying "mushrooms bought here." The Mendocino Mushroom Company, under the direction of Eric Schramm, collects and purchases wild mushrooms to ship to markets in San Francisco, New York, Japan, and Europe. Schramm started his company in 1985 while working for the Department of Forestry. Harvesting wild mushrooms requires certain responsibilities, says Schramm, who teaches his pickers to be careful not to cut the older spore-producing mushrooms and to "always cut the mushrooms so the mycelium under the ground is not disturbed, which would destroy future growth."

On the sweet side, Mendocino Chocolate Company has been rolling and dipping truffles on the coast since 1985. In Ukiah, Joan's Authentic Tasting English Toffee is another of the addictive product associated with Mendocino. Two stores specializing in the foods of local purveyors are Mendocino Bounty Specialty Marketplace, located in downtown Ukiah, and Carol Hall's Hot Pepper Jelly Company, in Fort Bragg.

ROUND MAN'S SMOKE HOUSE

ROUND MAN'S SMOKE HOUSE

412 North Main Street
Fort Bragg, CA 95437
(800) 545-2935; (707) 964-5954
fax (707) 964-3435

Owners: Marilyn Thorpe and
Stephen Rasmussen

ACCESS

Location: Downtown Fort Bragg,
off Main Street.

Hours: 10:00 A.M.-5:30 P.M. Monday-
Saturday; 10:00 A.M.-4:00 P.M.
Sunday; 10:00 A.M.-2:00 P.M.
Holidays. Closed July 4th,
Thanksgiving, Christmas Day.

Appointment necessary for tour? Yes.

AMENITIES

Products: Large line of smoked meats
and fish, including salmon, albacore,
Canadian bacon, chicken, pork chops,
pork loin, Louisiana Hot Links,
Jalapeño sausage, German sausages,
chorizo, linguisa, Turkey Thai sausage,
Turkey Sundial sausage, Turkey
Apple sausage, and jerky from beef
and salmon. Also smoked cheeses;
Round Man's Mustard, Round Man's
Mustard Hot.

Events: Mendocino Bounty; Winesong;
Art in the Gardens; and special in-
house tastings.

FROM LOOKING AT THE TINY STOREFRONT, IT'S HARD TO IMAGINE that a thousand pounds of meat are processed at Round Man's Smoke House every week. You will not meet nicer people than Stephen Rasmussen, his partner Marilyn Thorpe, who runs the retail store, and Steve Scudder, a former restaurant cook who has been in the meat business for over twelve years.

Round Man's has been a Fort Bragg business since 1989. In 1994, when the former owners wanted to retire, Rassmussen was initiating a change from teaching satellite communications at Ford Aerospace. He'd grown up in Sacramento, and Thorpe, a friend of his parents, had moved to the Mendocino Coast. They got to talking, decided they would go into business together, and bought Round Man's. The former owners trained them, and Scudder joined the team in 1995. They've enjoyed a steady growth through both mail order and retail sales.

Instant gratification motivates Rasmussen. "Each morning I start out with something raw, and it turns out beautiful by the end of the day," he says. What he starts out with are whole salmon or albacore tuna; sides, legs, or loins of pork; and odds and ends of high quality meat for the grinder. Smoked salmon, albacore, pork, ham, sausages, corned beef, and jerky are among his products.

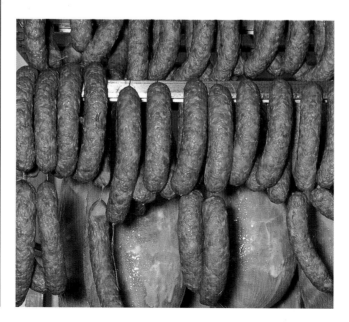

Stop by when Rassmussen isn't up to his elbows in sausage casings, or call ahead and make an appointment, and he'll show you how his special products take on their smoked delectability. Generally a tour is taken when the processing is finished. That means you get to see the equipment, the smoker, and the walk-in, which itself may be an eyefull of drying strips of salmon jerky or hanging sausages.

Rasmussen describes changes he has made in the processing and products. When most people think of smoked meats, they think salt. Here salt is lowered considerably so it isn't the first and only taste; spices, herbs, and chiles contribute more of the flavor in these premium products. He speeded up the smoking time, which he found makes the meats moister. Since taking over the business, he has added smoked chicken breasts, barbecued briskets, stuffed pork chops, and smoked duck sausages, with new items constantly being tried.

Getting involved in a meat business means the United States Department of Agriculture is also in the picture. A tiny separate office with a desk is reserved solely for the USDA inspector, who is on hand daily to make sure all the procedures are done according to the law and all the meat is inspected.

Some products have official ingredients that qualify them to have a certain label. For example, according to the USDA, to be labeled Polish sausage or Louisiana Hot Links, the products must contain prescribed generic spices in their formulas. On the other hand, specialty products such as Round Man's Sundial Turkey sausage can have a proprietary set of ingredients. In this case they include Fetzer Sundial Chardonnay.

Lean, quality cuts of meat are always used here. For the signature loins of pork, Rasmussen starts with whole loins and bones. He cuts and defats them himself, before seasoning and smoking them. The trim goes into a sausage mixture, which is primarily made with whole slabs of beef chuck and shoulders of pork. The turkey sausages are made only with breast and thigh meat, "no skins or by-products."

Each meat or fish has its own method of preparation before going in the smoker. The salmon comes in whole, and always fresh, from Canada or Alaska. Rasmussen fillets it and puts it in a brine for two-and-a-half to three hours. Then the fish is

taken out, rinsed, and put in the smoker. Afterwards it is cut and vacuum-packed. Albacore, Rasmussen's favorite, is done the same way as salmon. When making jerky from fish or meat, the process involves a long period of drying. Rasmussen does seventy-five to eighty pounds of turkey or salmon jerky at a time to meet its popular demand.

Particular care is given to making sausages. Most commercial sausage makers grind the meat two or three times, which makes an emulsified texture similar to hot dogs. All Round Man's sausages are single ground in a small grinder, a real hands-on process. Spices are mixed in by hand, and the meat is stuffed into natural casings. All the sausages are

linked by hand. Then, except for the breakfast and the Italian sausages, all are smoked.

Adjacent to the sterile room where the processing is done, a large walk-in refrigerator holds the day's products. A vacuum tumbler is also in the walk-in. Pork bellies (for bacon), hams, or corned beef are placed in it, and they are tumbled in specially spiced brines for up to six hours until the brine soaks in. "In the old days, this process took two weeks," Rasmussen says.

To him, the best part about the job is that every day is new. Some days he starts out packaging the previous day's smoking. Next he might make some custom sausage blends for one of the local restaurants. And then he starts his new orders for the day.

The local clientele and tourists alike are hooked on the products, and Marilyn loves catering to the people who come in the shop. Many buy the same sausage or smoked fish over and over, and she has gotten to know a fair number of visitors who return every year to attend events on the coast. "One family stocks gallons of the hot pickled links," she says.

Every day one or more of the products is cut up for samples. After the tour you can taste the results of the meticulous labors and judge for yourself whether all the extra touches are worth it. Then marvel at the number of products produced in such a small store.

THANKSGIVING COFFEE COMPANY

THANKSGIVING COFFEE COMPANY

South Harbor Drive
P.O. Box 1918
Fort Bragg, CA 95437
(800) 648-6491; (707) 964-0118
fax (707) 964-0351
Owners: Joan and Paul Katzeff

ACCESS

Location: From Highway 1, turn east on Highway 20 and make a left onto South Harbor Drive. Thanksgiving is on the left.

Hours: 9:00 A.M.-5:00 P.M. Monday-Friday; Closed Memorial Day, July 4, Yom Kippur, Thanksgiving, Rosh Hashanna, Christmas Day, New Year's Day

Appointment necessary for tour? Yes.

AMENITIES

Products: Coffees: 24 regular and 20 decaffeinated coffees; high caffeine Pony Express; an Organic Harvest line; and flavored coffees.

Teas: Premium teas.

Sales of coffee-related items? Yes, including logo cups and thermoses. Mail order available.

Events: Newsletter.

THE MENDOCINO COAST HAS ATTRACTED ENTREPRENEURS since the first traders came over 150 years ago. One business that has reached beyond the local region is Thanksgiving Coffee. Its story is one that parallels the social committment of the activists of the 1960s. It is also a model for sustaining a socially conscious business, hence their motto, "not just a cup, a just cup."

Thanksgiving Coffee Company started out in the garden of the Mendocino Hotel in 1972. Paul Katzeff had just moved to Mendocino from New York, where his love of coffee began as a mission and became a vocation. Having been raised on good fresh coffee, he found the only way to get it west of the Hudson was to roast his own. A trip back to New York netted an old coffee roaster lying idle in the back room of a grocery store in Greenwich Village. He carried the roaster to Mendocino in the trunk of his car. Right after his return, he met Joan, his partner and spouse-to-be. The two joined energies; they soon had the roaster fired up and were selling coffee from the Hotel.

Within a year the Katzeffs decided to expand their operations. They opened a restaurant called Thanksgiving in Fort Bragg, ten miles away. The coffee roaster continued to be the center of attention since it was set up in the middle of the dining room; the customers came as much for the fresh-brewed coffee as for the food. By 1974, Thanksgiving Coffee was being wholesaled locally, and the Katzeffs gave up the restaurant in favor of devoting full time to coffee roasting. They located the

budding business on the south side of Noyo Harbor, just below their present location.

In the ramshackle former fishermen's shack hanging over the Noyo River, Thanksgiving Coffee Company continued to grow for the next ten years. At first the green coffee beans came from distributors. As the company grew, Paul started sourcing beans himself. In 1985, he was president of the Specialty Coffee Association, an organization he helped found, when he met a coffee grower from Nicaragua who was trying to open American markets. Paul went to the grower's village, and the poverty and deforestation he saw there shook him up so much that when he returned he knew he had to make coffee a social justice issue. Thanksgiving Coffee instituted its "just cup" program, through which fifteen cents from every pound of green beans goes back to countries such as Nicuaragua, Costa Rica, Mexico, and Guatemala, where the coffee is grown. When enough money is collected, a village bank is set up to make loans for improvements. For example, in Costa Rica, where trees were being burned as fuel for drying coffee beans, seven thousand dollars was sent to set up a solar-powered coffee dryer. In a Mexican village nine thousand dollars was used to purchase mixers to prepare tortillas, a tedious task which previously began every morning at three. These projects are funded by Thanksgiving's organic coffees with the colorful Harvest labels.

"Social and environmental awareness is the path we have chosen to follow," says Joan. The path is defined by these self-help programs and the "coffee for peace" program in Nicaragua. Fifteen cents from every purchase of Nicaraguan coffee is donated to the Nicaraguan Center for Community Action, a group which promotes education about Nicaragua and coordinates volunteers to work on soil conservation and reforestation. All of these kickback programs are financed by Thanksgiving's growing line of organically produced coffees.

Taking a business from one hundred pounds a year in 1972 to 1.4 million pounds in 1995 has itself been an organic process. In the beginning, the Katzeffs did everything themselves with the help of high school kids and a few part-timers. The first full-time employee was hired in 1978 on the day Joan went into labor with her first child. Just when they were

making plans to remodel and expand the building on the River, the defunct Noyo River Restaurant just up the road came on the market. Thanksgiving Coffee was moved into the new facility in stages, finally connecting under one roof in 1985. Now the Katzeff's have forty employees; they added a daughter to the family in 1985.

Aromas from the new plant, like the old, still rise up the river when the coffee is roasting and permeate the air around the high Noyo River bridge. Taking a tour of the facility is an aromatic way to find out about the delicate nuances of coffee roasting. The tour begins with the bean-filled burlap bags shipped in from Latin and Central America, Africa, and Asia. The green beans (which look distinctively different depending on whether or not they are decaffeinated) are cleaned before roasting. The beans are blended before and after roasting, depending on the blend. For example, French and Vienna roasts are blends of several different green beans. House blends for restaurants such as the Albion River Inn and food stores such as Alfalfa's are usually blends of roasted beans. A hundred and fifty pounds at a time are roasted for an average of twenty minutes. Then they are cooled and funneled into bins to be packaged and labeled. Six packaging styles delineate classic regular coffee blends, decaffeinated coffees, specialty blends such as Half Caff and Kona Kulana Farms, coffees with single countries of origin, Organic Harvest roasts, and flavored coffees.

Organic beans are compeletely segregated during processing, which means special containers are labeled just for them throughout the facility. When flavored coffees are roasted, they add their own scented essence to the air. One day it might be vanilla, another hazelnut. Between 15 and 20 percent of Thanksgiving's coffee sales are for flavored coffee. Extensive tasting is done in the cupping room to maintain the quality and consistency of roasts.

In 1989, Thanksgiving added a line of premium teas under the name Royal Gardens. Whole-leaf teas are packaged in beautiful foil wraps. Some of the tea is packed in the most unique tea bags in the industry. Since whole leaves, unlike crushed shakes, expand when wet, they would tear traditional paper tea bags. By making the bags of cloth, which expands, the more flavorful whole tea leaves can be brewed. In addition to Ceylon, Jasmine, and Earl Grey teas, Royal Gardens has a black tea, called Russian Caravan, and a green tea, called Goddess. The Goddess tea comes from a small Chinese village co-op. The tea was discovered by the Katzeffs in 1980, when they went on a Chinese exchange trip with a group from Mendocino in support of a cooperative educational and farming venture in the village.

When Joan and Paul started in the coffee business, there were thirty companies in the United States roasting coffee; now there are more than eight hundred specialty coffee roasters. "When we go to a trade show now," says Joan, "we feel like grandparents in the industry." Such hip grandparents are setting an example for generations to come.

ALEX R. THOMAS & COMPANY

AFTER WINE GRAPES, THE FIRST FRUIT CROP OF MENDOCINO is pears. Most commercial pears are grown in the fertile Yokayo Valley around Ukiah. The biggest packing shed in California is run by one of the oldest agricultural families in the county, the Thomases.

You can see the gigantic Alex R. Thomas packing plant set among the pear orchards on the east side of Highway 101, near the turnoff to Boonville. It is a family-run business begun by Alex Thomas in 1919.

The Thomas story is also the history of commercial pear growing in Ukiah. Prior to Alex's arrival, in the mid-1800s, many Italians settled in this fertile valley because it resembled northern Italy. They planted what was familiar to them: grapes and pears. The climate of hot days and warm nights made the valley a premium environment for growing both. In addition to the fruit, many acres along the Russian River from Ukiah to Hopland were planted with hops, an important ingredient for beer. Hop cultivation declined after the First World War, and pears and grapes took their place. In 1919, as Thomas and Cunningham, Alex and a partner started marketing pears outside the area. They had to pack the pears in ice in their trucks until refrigerated transportation improved the process.

Now in a state-of-the-art facility, this multimillion dollar business is run by Thomas's children. The oldest son, Tom, manages the hundred-thousand-square-foot packing plant.

Dan is the financial manager, and John and Steve are two of the growers.

While tours are available by appointment all year long, the packing plant is empty except for August and early September. In those two months, an average of 33,000 tons of pears are processed. Not so long ago, the majority of the pears were sent to canneries. Now about 60 percent are sold fresh, which indicates a change in consumer eating habits as well as the ability to store pears for up to six months. Bartletts account for 90 percent of the production, Boscs 7 percent, Reds 3 percent; a tiny number of Comice pears are grown, most of which go to Hickory Farms for their fruit-of-the-month club.

Pears grown in Ukiah are called "mountain pears" to be differentiated from "valley pears" grown in the Sacramento valley. The first pears each season come from Sacramento, but they are difficult to store and the "flavor is not as intense as a mountain pear," say local growers. Mendocino and Lake counties are always the first on the market with mountain pears.

In mid-March, the orchards along Highway 101 are in full bloom. It takes about 120 days for the pears to be ready for picking. Since pears ripen from the inside out, they are picked just as they begin to ripen. If pears ripen on the tree they rot, and any pears you might have bought that were brown in the middle were picked too late. Like grapes, they have to be picked when the sugar level and the flesh firmness, or pressure (both measured and checked frequently), are just right. Another similarity to grapes is that, as the orchards get older, they bear more and better pears. One of the orchards the Thomases process is over 130 years old.

Once picked, the pears are cooled immediately, then washed, graded, and packed. Since they all come in at once, the time to visit the Thomas Packing Plant is in August, when 750 full-time employees race the clock to get the pears sorted and sent to their appropriate markets. On one side of the plant, seven conveyor belts are manned by employees who attend "sorting school" before going on the line. At the peak of harvest, 175 nine-hundred-pound bins are sorted each hour. Pears destined for canning go one way and those to be eaten fresh move along belts to the packers. Most pears are packed in layers in boxes, but the very best are hand-wrapped in a square of tissue that is imprinted with the Thomas logo, a commitment to the quality, and the signature of each of the eighteen growers. The perfect pear, says Tom Thomas, is one that has been stored at thirty degrees for two weeks and then allowed to come to room temperature. That's what gives the best flavor and buttery texture. These are the pears packed in boxes labeled "Mendocino Gold."

Temperature and storage are major concerns to pear packers, who want to provide the best product for as long as possible. As the demand for canning pears drops, the attention given to storage and to keeping up with the consumer demand for high quality fresh fruit rises. At the Thomas plant, an acre of refrigerated building houses rooms of various temperatures designed to cool the pears down as much as possible to slow their ripening, making them available for as long as six months.

MENDOCINO COUNTY GRAPES AND WINES

Mendocino County has one of the coolest growing climates in California. The average summer temperatures range from forty-five to ninety-five degrees Farenheit. The average rainfall is 36.6 inches. Vineyards were first planted in the 1850s. By 1910 there were 5,800 acres planted to vines; in 1994 there were 13,155, of which 3,000 were organic. In 1995, Mendocino had the most organic vineyard acreage in the state.

There are nine distinctive viticultural appellations in the county, including the designation Mendocino. In the southeast part of the county is McDowell Valley, which, in 1982, was one of the earliest regions to receive official American Viticultural Appellation (AVA) status. Actually a bench, its elevation ranges from 850 to 1,200 feet and harbors a Mediterranean climate that supports Rhone-style varietals like Syrah and Grenache, which have grown there for 100 years.

Sanel Valley is the region which extends south of Ukiah and around Hopland. Insulated by a narrow canyon to the south and watered by the Russian River, the climate is hotter than many other parts of the county. It is perfect for Chardonnay, Sauvignon Blanc, Cabernet Sauvignon, and Merlot.

Ukiah Valley, in what is also known as Yokayo Valley, encompasses about twenty miles along the Russian River, extending from Sanel Valley to Redwood Valley. Hillsides and benchlands support Zinfandel and Cabernet Sauvignon, while the river plain is better for Chardonnay and Sauvignon Blanc.

Redwood Valley, to the north of Ukiah, is known for rolling hills, red soil, and some of the oldest vineyards in the county. Chardonnay, Sauvignon Blanc, Zinfandel, Cabernet Sauvignon, and Petite Sirah grow here.

Potter Valley is twelve miles northeast of Ukiah. It was established as an AVA in 1983 and supports Sauvignon Blanc, Chardonnay, and Riesling grapes.

Cole Ranch was established as an AVA in 1983. It is a sixty-acre, single proprietor appellation southwest of Ukiah with elevations ranging from 1,400 to 1,600 feet. Cabernet Sauvignon and Riesling grow here.

On the southwest side of the county is Anderson Valley. Cooled by its proximity to the Pacific Ocean, mornings are often foggy and afternoons hot. Established as an AVA in 1983, it is known for Chardonnay, Pinot Noir, Gewürztraminer and ridge-top Zinfandel. Because the Chardonnay and Pinot Noir make such excellent sparkling wine, I like to call Anderson Valley the "Champagne" of California.

To the east of Anderson Valley is Yorkville Highlands, which borders the northern end of Sonoma's Alexander Valley. Hot summers bring out the best in Cabernet Sauvignon and Sauvignon Blanc.

The following is a list of wines and grapes from Mendocino County.

Barbera: A red hearty grape from the Piedmont region of Italy. Flavor is rich and tannic rather than fruity. Not many acres are planted anymore; Domaine St. Gregory and Parducci make small amounts.

Burgundy: A generic term for red wine in the United States, not to be confused with wine from the French region of Bourgogne. Most producers are substituting "Red Table Wine" for the old designation. Flavor can run from dry to slightly sweet.

Cabernet Franc: A popular grape for blending with Cabernet Sauvignon; tastes lighter and fruitier than Cabernet. About seventy-one acres are planted in Mendocino.

Cabernet Sauvignon: Makes the world's most famous and finest wines. One of the last grapes to harvest, the wine is known for its aging potential and its rich tannic to velvety flavors. Grows best on hot hillsides. There are 130 acres in Mendocino.

Carignane: Once the most common red grape in California, it does well in warm areas; 896 acres are dedicated to it in this county. The color is dark and the flavor is light. Parducci produces it as a varietal.

Charbono: A red grape, most likely of French origin; makes a medium-bodied pleasant wine; Pacific Star Winery on the Mendocino coast makes 600 cases from grapes grown on sixty acres in Calpella.

Chardonnay: One of the world's finest white grapes for dry and sparkling wines, this is the white Burgundy from France. Over 4,060 acres are planted here. Flavor descriptors include oaky, buttery, intensely creamy, and fruity. In Anderson Valley, it is often described as flinty.

Chenin Blanc: Well regarded for its light crispness and dry to honey-like sweetness, this is a white grape with a loyal, but not huge following. Grows on 394 acres here. Husch Vineyards is known for this wine.

Cinsault: A red grape with full flavor and deep color, this Rhône variety is also spelled Cinsaut. A few acres are planted in McDowell Valley.

French Colombard: The most widely planted grape in California, 335 acres support it in Mendocino. It is usually blended with Chenin Blanc or other grapes to make a generic white wine with a light, fruity flavor.

Fumé Blanc: The name given to dry-style Sauvignon Blanc by Robert Mondavi in the 1960s, it is now used by many other producers of this popular wine. See Sauvignon Blanc.

Gamay: Confusion reigns about the relationship between this grape and the Gamay Beaujolais. Both are light and thin in flavor. Seventy-two acres of it grow in Mendocino.

Gamay Beaujolais: A light red wine grape that is declining in popularity in California. A relative of the popular Pinot Noir, 254 acres are grown here.

Gewürztraminer: The name comes from the German word for spice and refers to its aroma and flavor, which runs from dry (about 0.5 percent residual sugar) to quite sweet. A wonderful aperitif as well as a complement to spicy Asian food. The best of the dry ones come from Anderson Valley; a total of 297 acres are grown in Mendocino.

Grenache: A red grape popular in the south of France and in Spain; as the popularity of Rhône wines rises, more of this grape may be seen. Usually made into dry rosés with a slightly fruity aftertaste. It has been growing in McDowell Valley since 1919, where twenty of the thirty eight acres in the county are planted.

Grey or Gray Riesling: Nineteen acres of this thin-tasting white grape are growing, probably for export to wineries out of the area.

Johannisberg Riesling: The true name is White Riesling. A distinctively flavored grape, it is the darling of many wine aficionados for its versatility in being made bone dry or in a slightly fruity style. If left on the vine and attacked by the sweetness-inducing mold known as botrytis, an extremely sweet late-harvest version is made. Mendocino has 153 acres; Greenwood Ridge and Navarro Vineyards make good examples.

Late harvest: Denotes a dessert-sweet wine, usually made from grapes attacked by a sweetness-inducing mold known as botrytis. Popular examples are made from Riesling, Gewürztraminer, Muscat Canelli, Semillon, Sauvignon Blanc, or Zinfandel grapes.

Marsanne: A white grape producing wine with light floral aromas, crisp clean finish, and big texture in the mouth. McDowell Valley Vineyards has three acres, planted in 1992.

Merlot: This is the second most popular red grape in the Bordeaux and is often blended with Cabernet Sauvignon to give it more of a fruity and supple character. Here it is becoming a popular varietal and supply can't keep up with demand; 366 acres are growing with more being planted all the time.

Mourvèdre: A red grape from the south of France with a name like a Shakespearian character. As the Rhône varietals increase in popularity in California, more of this grape will be found both blended and as a varietal. It has a deep rich color and slightly tart flavor.

Nebbiolo: One of the two top red grapes (with Sangiovese) in the Piedmont region of Italy, where it is known as Barolo. There are small plantings in the county where the Italian influence is strong. It makes a wine that is a critic's delight in roundness and complexity.

Petite Sirah: A California name given to Durif, a French grape; 301 acres of it exist in Mendocino, much of it old vines producing inky, peppery, slightly tannic wine that goes well with pasta, meat, and potatoes.

Pinot Blanc: Twenty-six acres of this mellow dry grape are planted in Mendocino. It makes a wonderfully versatile white wine.

Pinot Meunier: Related to Pinot Noir, with deeper fruity flavor, it is most commonly blended with Pinot Noir and Chardonnay for sparkling wine. Handley Cellars bottles it as a varietal.

Pinot Noir: A versatile grape perfect as the foundation for sparkling wine and as a varietal on its own; 556 acres are growing in Mendocino. Much of it is in Anderson Valley, where it is picked early and made into sparkling wine or allowed to ripen to make full-flavored varietals with the aroma and aftertaste of blackberries and raspberries.

Port: Sweet, fortified wine made from Syrah, Petite Sirah, Zinfandel, and other red grapes; perfect for serving after dinner on a blustery night.

Roussane: A northern Rhône white varietal similar to Marsanne. McDowell Valley has 1.2 acres of it.

Rosé: Pink wine made from red grapes that are harvested and kept with their skins long enough to extract a little color. Usually has fresh, fruity flavor and is not always sweet. Rhône-style rosé is quite dry and goes with many dishes, especially seafood and poultry.

Sangiovese: The principle grape in Italy's famous Chianti is attracting attention as a great food wine. Obester bottles it in a non-traditional flat-sided bottle.

Sauvignon Blanc: California's second-favorite white wine grape makes an all-purpose wine most commonly described as grassy, but that characteristic is mellowed out of most examples by various winemaking techniques and blending with Semillon. There are 1,049 acres in Mendocino. It does well in the Yorkville Highlands and Sanel Valley.

Semillon: About twenty eight acres of this white grape are planted in Mendocino. The bland flavor makes it better for blending (with Sauvignon Blanc) than bottling as a varietal, unless you count its reputation in France. There it becomes the famous Sauternes when botrytis turns it opulently sweet for dessert wine.

Sparkling wine: If the label reads *méthode champenoise*, this is champagne. Most wineries, in deference to the French law allowing Champagne on the label only if the wine comes from the Champagne region, call their bottle-fermented output sparkling wine. Mendocino sparklers, most from Anderson Valley, are made from blends of Chardonnay and Pinot Noir and sometimes a little Pinot Meunier. Flavors range from dry (brut) to sweet (sec and demi-sec).

Syrah: Another of the Rhône varietals, it promises to get increased attention because of its peppery and blackcurrant flavors. A complement to hearty Mediterranean-style pizza and pastas, 122 acres are in Mendocino, 72 of which are in McDowell Valley.

Viognier: A white Rhône varietal which is gaining fast in popularity. The flavor runs from dry with the hint of peaches and apricots to tart-like grapefruit. It has the distinction of being blended into red Rhône wines. Nineteen acres have been in McDowell Valley since 1989; Fetzer has thirty seven acres.

Zinfandel: Of uncertain origins, Zinfandel is known and loved as California's adopted varietal, and Sonoma County is its mother. Hundred-year-old vines are also found on Mendocino's hillsides, where most of the 1,782 acres grow. The old vines are revered for the great body and depth that accompany the already spicy and berry-rich flavors of the robust wine.

Sources for this list include Mendocino County's wineries, the Mendocino County Winegrowers Association, Mendocino Department of Agriculture, *The New Connoisseur's Book of California Wines*, by Norman Roby and Charles Olken, and *The New Frank Schoonmaker Encyclopedia of Wine*, by Alexis Bespaloff.

RESOURCES

Note: all resources are in the 707 telephone area code unless indicated otherwise.

FOR EDUCATION

Mendocino Art Center
45200 Little Lake Street
Mendocino, CA 95460
937-5818

Ecology Action
Common Ground Mini-Farm
5798 Ridgewood Road
Willits, CA 95490-9730
459-0150
fax 459-5409

Emandal, A Farm on a River
16500 Hearst Post Office Road
Willits, CA 95490
(800) 262-9597; 459-5439

FOR HISTORY

Anderson Valley Historical
   Museum
Highway 128
P.O. Box 676
Boonville, CA 95415
895-2379

Ford House
Main Street
P.O. Box 1387
Mendocino, CA 95437
937-5397

Fort Building
430 North Franklin Street
Fort Bragg, CA 95437
961-2825

Grace Hudson Museum &
   Sun House
431 South Main Street
Ukiah, CA 95482
462-3370

Guest House Museum
343 North Main Street
Fort Bragg, CA 95437
961-2840

Held-Poage Research Library
603 West Perkins Street
Ukiah, CA 95482
462-6969

Kelly House Museum
45007 Albion Street
P.O. Box 922
Mendocino, CA 95460

Mendocino County
   Historical Society
603 West Perkins
Ukiah, CA 95482
462-6969

Mendocino County Museum
400 East Commercial Street
Willits, CA 95490
459-2736

Point Arena Lighthouse
   & Museum
Lighthouse Road
Point Arena, CA 94568
882-2777

Pomo Visitors Center
North Lake Mendocino
Marina Drive
Lake Mendocino
Ukiah, CA 95482
485-8685

FOR GRAPE GROWING AND RANCHING

Mendocino County
   Cattlemen's Association
16100 N. Higway 101 #59
Willits, CA 95490
459-6055

Mendocino County
   Farm Bureau
303 Talmage Road
Ukiah, CA 95482
462-6664

Mendocino Winegrowers
   Alliance
P.O. Box 1409
Ukiah, CA 95482-1409
468-1409

Mendocino Woolgrowers
   Association
Bo Peeps
P.O. Box 548
Boonville, CA 95415
895-0548

FOR TOURING

Hopland Chamber
   of Commerce
Hopland, CA 95449
744-1404; 744-1171

Fort Bragg-Mendocino Coast
   Chamber of Commerce
332 North Main Street
P.O. Box 1141
Fort Bragg, CA 95437
(800) 726-2780; 961-6300

Mendocino County
   Tourism Board
239 South Main St.
Willits, CA 95490
459-7910

FOR WINE AND FOOD EVENTS

Anderson Valley Winegrowers
   Association
Box 63
Philo, CA 95466

Hopland Winery Association
c/o Brutocao
P.O. Box 780
Hopland, CA 95449

Fort Bragg-Mendocino Coast
   Chamber of Commerce
   (see *For Touring*)

Mendocino Bounty
462-3306

Winesong!
700 River Drive
Fort Bragg, CA 95437
961-4688

BOOKS

*Boontling, An American
   Lingo* (1991)
by Charles C. Adams
Mountain House Press
P.O. Box 353
Philo, CA 95466

Cafe Beaujolais (1984)
by Margaret Fox and John Bear
Ten Speed Press
P.O. Box 7123
Berkeley, CA 94707

*The Glove Box Guide to
   the Mendocino Coast:
   Lodging, Eating,
   Sights, History,
   Activities & More*
   (1995)
by Bob Lorentzen
Bored Feet Publications
P.O. Box 1832
Mendocino, CA 95460

*Good Thyme Herb Blends
Cookbook* (1995)
by Debra Dawson
Good Thyme Press
P.O. Box 975
Mendocino, CA 95460

*The Hiker's Hip Pocket
Guide to the Mendocino
Coast* (1987)
by Bob Lorentzen
Bored Feet Publications
P.O. Box 1832
Mendocino, CA 95460

Mendocino Coast Bike Rides
(1996)
by Bob Lorentzen
Bored Feet Publications
P.O. Box 1832
Mendocino, CA 95460

*Sea Vegetable Gourmet
Cookbook and
Wildcrafter's Guide*
(1995)
by Eleanor and John Lewellan
Mendocino Sea Vegetable Co.
P.O. Box 1265
Mendocino, CA 95460

MAGAZINES/NEWSPAPERS

Anderson Valley Advertiser
12451 Anderson Valley Way
Boonville, CA 95415
895-3016

A & E Magazine
Mendocino Art Center
45200 Little Lake Street
P.O. Box 765
Mendocino, CA 95460
937-5818

Coast Magazine
P.O. Box 695
Gualala, CA 95445
(800) 984-3422; 884-4019

Fort Bragg Advocate-News
450 N. Franklin
Fort Bragg, CA 95437
964-5642

Independent Coast Observer
P.O. Box 1200
Gualala, CA 95455
884-3501

Mendocino Beacon
P.O. Box 225
Mendocino, CA 95460
937-5874

Mendocino Coast Travelers Guide
P.O. Box 595
Little River, CA 95456
937-2105

Mendocino Visitor Magazine
P.O. Box 1374
Eureka, CA 95502
443-4887

Outlook
10525 Ford St.
P.O. Box 2450
Mendocino, CA 95460
937-2906

Real Estate Magazine
155A Cypress St.
Fort Bragg, CA 95437
964-1318

Steppin' Out
Francis Publications
P.O. Box 1458
Fort Bragg, CA 95437
964-4193

Ukiah Daily Journal
590 S. School Street
Ukiah, CA 95482
468-0123

Willits News
1424 N. Main Street
Willits, CA 95490
459-4643

CERTIFIED FARMERS' MARKETS

Redwood Empire Farmers
Market Association of
Mendocino County
P.O. Box 68
Calpella, CA 95418

SUNDAY

Laytonville:
June-October
2:00-5:00 P.M.
Good Food Store
984-8805

Willits:
May-October
1:00-4:00 P.M.
City Park
459-5470

TUESDAY

Ukiah:
Mid-May to mid-October
3:00-6:00 P.M.
School & Clay Streets
743-1669

WEDNESDAY

Fort Bragg:
May-October
3:30-5:30 P.M.
E. Laurel and Franklin Streets
964-0536

THURSDAY

Willits:
May-November
3:00-6:00 P.M.
City Park
459-5470

FRIDAY

Mendocino:
May-October
12:00-2:00 P.M.
Howard Street, South
937-3322

SATURDAY

Boonville:
Mid-May to mid-October
9:00 A.M.-12:00 P.M.
Boonville Hotel
895-3957

EVENTS

Community Breakfasts:

Grange: First Sunday of each month at Inglenook, 6 miles north of Fort Bragg on Highway 1.
8:00 A.M.–1:00 P.M.

Moose: Third Sunday of each month on Sherwood Road, 1½ miles east of Main on Oak, Fort Bragg.
8:00 A.M.–Noon.

Whitesboro Grange: Fourth Sunday of each month, 32510 Navarro Ridge Road, Albion.
8:00 A.M.–Noon.

Legion of the Moose Champagne Breakfast: Fifth Sunday of the month Sherwood Road, 1½ miles east of Main on Oak, Fort Bragg.
8:00 A.M.–Noon

Fort Bragg First Friday. Artist openings and gallery receptions 5:30 P.M.–8:30 P.M. First Friday of each month. Downtown Fort Bragg.
964-0807

Mendocino Second Saturday. Artist openings & gallery receptions. Mendocino village.
5:30 P.M.–9:00 P.M.

January
Lion's Club Crab Feed. Redwood Empire Fairgrounds. Ukiah. 462-3884

February
Chocolate Festival, Gualala Arts Center. 884-1138

March
Mendocino Whale Festival: Wine tasting, chowder tasting, and more. Mendocino, 961-6300. First weekend.

Fort Bragg Whale Festival: Seafood chowder tasting; Microbrewer Beerfest, and more. Fort Bragg, 961-6300. Third weekend.

April
Invitation to Hopland. Winery open houses with food and music. Third weekend.
744-1066

May
Historic House and Building Tour. Benefit for the Kelly House, first weekend.
937-5971

Willits Annual Community Festival. Willits. 459-7910

Cinco de Mayo. Annual Mexican fiesta in downtown Fort Bragg. 961-6300

Garcia Fire & Rescue Barbecue. Point Arena.

June
Taste of Redwood Valley. Winery open houses. Father's Day weekend.
485-1221

Albion-Little River Fire Department Sirloin BBQ; Little River Airport. 937-0496

Mendocino Coast Writers Conference, College of the Redwoods. 961-1001

July
Mendocino 4th of July Parade. 961-6300

World's Largest Salmon Barbecue. Noyo Harbor. Saturday closest to July 4th.
964-6535

Woolgrower's Barbecue and Sheepdog Trials. Boonville Fairgrounds. 895-3011

Mendocino Music Festival. Two-week long program.
937-2044

Frontier Days and Rodeo. Willits. 459-7910

August
Art in the Gardens. Art, music, wine and food, Mendocino Coast Botanical Gardens.
964-4352

Mendocino Bounty. Showcase tasting of food and beverages. Fetzer Vineyards, Hopland.
462-3306

Mendocino Art Center Summer Fair. Mendocino.
937-5818

Art in the Redwoods Festival. Gualala Art Center. 884-1138

September
Paul Bunyan Days. Fort Bragg. Labor Day weekend. 961-6300

Redwood Empire Fair. Ukiah Fair Grounds. 462-3884

Winesong! Auction, wine and food tasting benefit for Mendocino Coast Hospital, Mendocino Coast Botanical Gardens. 961-4688

Mendocino County Fair and Apple Show. Boonville Fair Grounds. 895-3011

October
Abalone Festival. Abalone Cook-off, Van Damme State Park. 937-4016

Country Pumpkinfest. Downtown Ukiah.

November
Mushroom Festival. Exhibits and demonstrations. Fort House Visitors Center, Mendocino. 937-5397

Thanksgiving Fair. Mendocino Art Center. 937-5818

December
Mendocino Christmas. Events, inn tours, teas, tree lighting. 961-6300

Fort Bragg Hometown Christmas. Tree lighting, parade. 961-6300

Celebrity Cooks and Kitchens Tour. Mendocino. 961-6300

ASSOCIATED VINTAGE GROUP

P.O. Box 548
Hopland, CA 95449
744-1700
No tours or tasting

BRUTOCAO CELLARS

7000 Highway 128
Philo, CA 95466
895-2152
Tasting: 10:00 A.M.-6:00 P.M.
daily
Picnic area: Yes

CLAUDIA SPRINGS WINERY

P.O. Box 348
Philo, CA 95466
895-3926
Tasting: By appointment

DOMAINE ST. GREGORY
& MONTE VOLPE

4921 Eastside Road
Ukiah, CA 95482
463-1532
Tasting: By appointment or
at Redwood Valley Cellars

DUNCAN PEAK VINEYARDS

14500 Mountain House Road
Hopland, CA 95449
744-1129; 415/893-1000
Tasting: By appointment

DUNNEWOOD VINEYARDS

2399 North State Street
Ukiah, CA 95482
462-2985
Tasting: 10:00 A.M.-5:00 P.M.
daily
Picnic area: Yes

EDMEADES ESTATE/
KENDALL-JACKSON

5500 Highway 128
Philo, CA 95466
895-3009
Tasting: By appointment

ELIZABETH VINEYARDS

8591 Colony Drive
Redwood Valley, CA 95470
485-0957
Tasting: By appointment or
at Redwood Valley Cellars

FETZER VINEYARDS

Wine and Visitor Center
13601 Eastside Road
Hopland, CA 95449
744-1250

MENDOCINO TASTING ROOM

45070 Main Street
Mendocino, CA 95460
937-6190
Tasting: See entry in book

FREY VINEYARDS

14000 Tomki Road
Redwood Valley, CA 95470
485-5177
Tasting: By appointment
Picnic area: Yes

GABRIELLI WINERY

10950 West Road
Redwood Valley, CA 95470
485-1221
Tasting: 10:00 A.M.-5:00 P.M.
daily
Picnic area: Yes

GERMAIN-ROBIN
ALAMBIC, INC.

3001 South State Street #31
Ukiah, CA 95482
462-0314; 462-3221
Tasting: Sales at Ukiah address

GREENWOOD RIDGE
VINEYARDS

5501 Highway 128
Philo, CA 95466
895-2002
Tasting: daily
10:00 A.M.-6:00 P.M. summer;
10:00 A.M.-5:00 P.M. winter
Picnic area: Yes

HANDLEY CELLARS

3151 Highway 128
Philo, CA 95466
895-3876
Tasting: daily
11:00 A.M.-6:00 P.M. summer;
11:00 A.M.-5:00 P.M. winter
Picnic area: Yes

HIDDEN CELLARS

1500 Ruddick-
Cunningham Road
Ukiah, CA 95482
462-0301
Tasting: By appointment

HUSCH VINEYARDS

4400 Highway 128
Philo, CA 95466
895-3216
Tasting:
10:00 A.M.-6:00 P.M. summer;
10:00 A.M.-5:00 P.M. winter
Picnic area: Yes

JEPSON VINEYARDS

10400 South Highway 101
Ukiah, CA 95482
468-8936
Tasting: 10:00 A.M.-5:00 P.M.
daily
Picnic area: Yes

KONRAD ESTATE WINERY

3620 Road B
Redwood Valley, CA 95470
485-0323
Tasting: 10:00 A.M.-5:00 P.M.
daily
Picnic area: Yes

LAZY CREEK VINEYARDS

4601 Highway 128
Philo, CA 95466
895-3623
Visitors: By appointment
Picnic area: Yes

LOLONIS WINERY

2901 Road B
Redwood Valley, CA 95470
485-8027
Visitors: By appointment

MARIAH VINEYARDS & WINES

P.O. Box 744
Point Arena, CA 95468
882-2243

MARTZ VINEYARDS

20799 Highway 128
Yorkville, CA 95494
895-2334
Tasting: 10:00 A.M.-6:00 P.M.
Friday, Saturday, Sunday
Picnic area: Yes

McDOWELL VALLEY
VINEYARDS

3811 Highway 175
P.O. Box 449
Hopland, CA 95449
744-1053
Tasting: By appointment
Picnic area: Yes

MILANO WINERY
14594 South Highway 101
Hopland, CA 95449
744-1396
Tasting: 10:00 A.M.-5:00 P.M.
  daily
Picnic area: Yes

MOUNTAIN HOUSE
WINERY & LODGE
38999 Highway 128
Cloverdale, CA 95425
894-2238; 578-0769
Tasting: 9:00 A.M.-5:00 P.M.
  Wednesday-Sunday
Picnic area: Yes

NAVARRO VINEYARDS
& WINERY
5601 Highway 128
Philo, CA 95466
895-3686
Tasting:
  10:00 A.M.-6:00 P.M. summer;
  10:00 A.M.-5:00 P.M. winter
Picnic area: Yes

OBESTER WINERY
9200 Highway 128
Philo, CA 95466
895-3814
Tasting: 10:00 A.M.-5:00 P.M.
  daily
Picnic area: Yes

PACIFIC STAR WINERY
33000 North Highway 1
Fort Bragg, CA 95437
964-1155
Visitors: By appointment

PARDUCCI WINE CELLARS
501 Parducci Road
Ukiah, CA 95482
462-5357
Tasting: 9:00 A.M.-5:00 P.M.
  daily
Picnic area: Yes

PEPPERWOOD SPRINGS
VINEYARDS & WINERY
1200 Holmes Road
Philo, CA 95466
895-2920
Visitors: By appointment

REDWOOD VALLEY CELLARS
TASTING ROOM
7051 North State Street
Ukiah, CA 95482
485-0322
Tasting:
  9:00 A.M.-6:00 P.M. summer;
  9:00 A.M.-5:00 P.M. winter
Picnic area: Yes

ROEDERER ESTATE
4501 Highway 128
Philo, CA 95466
895-3876
Tasting: 11:00 A.M.-5:00 P.M.
  daily

SCHARFFENBERGER CELLARS
8501 Highway 128
Philo, CA 95466
895-2957
Tasting: 11:00 A.M.-5:00 P.M.
  daily
Picnic area: Yes

SOUZAO CELLARS
19750 Highway 128
Yorkville, CA 95494
895-2733

WHALER VINEYARDS
6200 Eastside Road
Ukiah, CA 95482
462-6355

YORKVILLE CELLARS
Mile Marker 40.4
  Highway 128
P.O. Box 3
Yorkville, CA 95494
894-9177
Tasting: 11:00 A.M.-5:00 P.M.
  daily
Picnic area: Yes

ZELLARBACH WINERY
2350 McNab Ranch Road
Ukiah, CA 95482
462-2423
Tasting: By appointment

A Directory of Mendocino County Food and Beverage Resources

ACKERMAN'S FOODS
P.O. Box 486
Mendocino, CA 95460
961-1351
cakes; mustard

ALEX R. THOMAS & COMPANY
P.O. Box 748
Ukiah, CA 95482
462-4716
wholesale pears

ANDERSON VALLEY
BREWING COMPANY
14081 Highway 128
P.O. Box 505
Boonville, CA 95415
(800) 207-2337; 895-2353
micro-brews

THE APPLE FARM
18501 Greenwood Road
Philo, CA 95466
895-2333
retail & mail order: apple juice,
  chutneys, jams, cider syrup,
  cider vinegar, apples

BIG RIVER COFFEE COMPANY
P.O. Box 6
Mendocino, CA 95460
937-4419
whole bean and organic coffees

BRUCE BREAD BAKERY
P.O. Box 164
Boonville, CA 95415
895-2148
whole grain breads, baguettes,
  pizza crusts

BUTLER CHERRY RANCH
Highway 253
Ukiah, CA 95482
462-4650
Bing, Lambert, Royal Anne
  cherries; figs, plums, and
  grapes

CAFE BEAUJOLAIS
BAKERY & BRICKERY
961 Ukiah Street
P.O. Box 730
Mendocino, CA 95460
937-0443
mail order panforte, fruitcake,
  waffle mix, hot chocolate mix,
  BBQ sauce, jams, Austrian
  seed bread

CAITO FISHERIES
P.O. Box 1370
Fort Bragg, CA 95437
964-6368
wholesale seafood

THE CANDY KITCHEN
92 South State St.
Willits, CA 95490
459-2776
complete line of homemade
  candy and ice cream

THE CHEESECAKE LADY
P.O. Box 584
Hopland, CA 95449
744-1312
retail and mail order
  cheesecakes

COMPROMISE
MOUNTAIN RANCH
2960 Black Hawk Road
Willits, CA 95490
468-6914
freezer lambs, pygmy goats,
  Thanksgiving turkeys

COTTON WOOD ACRES/
LITTLE RED HOUSE HERBS
22640 East Side Road
Willits, Ca 95490
459-4401; 459-9406
organically grown milk-fed
  lambs; organic culinary herbs;
  fresh eggs; rabbits

COVELO ORGANIC
VEGETABLES
23090 Hopper Lane
Covelo, CA 95428
983-6562
melons, produce

DRUMMOND FARMS
P.O. Box 1694
Mendocino, CA 95460
937-1758
fresh fruit chutneys

EAGLE ROCK GOURMET LAMB
42400 Highway 128
Cloverdale, CA 95425
894-2814
mail order lamb

EMMANDEL—
A FARM ON A RIVER
16500 Hearst Post Office Road
Willitts, 95490
800/262-9597; 459-5439
jams, pickles, sauces, whole
  grain mixes, herbs plus summer camps for kids, family
  and country vacations and
  workshops

FULLER'S FINE HERBS
P.O. Box 1344
Mendocino, CA 95460
937-0860

GOOD THYME HERB COMPANY
P.O. Box 975
Mendocino, CA 95460
964-0509
herb blends, cookbook

GOWAN'S OAK TREE
FRUIT STAND
6600 Highway 128
Philo, CA 95466
895-3353
large variety of fruits and
  vegetables by the pound
  and lug

GREAT CHEFS OF MENDOCINO
P.O. Box 771
Hopland, CA 95449
800/982-1800; 468-5538
mail-order Mendocino County
  products and gift packs

HENNE'S CANDY
582 North State St.
Ukiah, CA 95482
462-5661
homemade ice cream and
  candies

HOT PEPPER JELLY COMPANY
330 North Main Street
Fort Bragg, CA 95437
800/892-4823; 961-1422
retail and mail order hot pepper
  jellies, mustards, jams, chutneys and a long line of
  Mendocino County foodstuffs

JOAN'S ENGLISH TOFFEE
1450 Redemeyer Road
Ukiah, CA 95482
462-0653
English toffee

JOHNSON ORCHARDS
P.O. Box 748
Ukiah, CA 95482
462-7560
pears, salsa

KAITLAND CREEK RANCH
2340 Boonville Road
Ukiah,CA 95482
468-8416
raspberries

LITTLE RIVER INN MUSTARD
P.O. Box 503
Little River, CA 95456
937-5942
whole grain and garlic mustards

MARIMAX FARMS
10560 Main Street
Potter Valley, CA 95469
743-1669
produce, including
    pickling cucumbers sold at
    farmers' markets

MARTIN ORGANIC FARM
P.O. Box 301
Comptche, CA 95427
937-2274
organic produce

MCFADDEN FARM
16000 Powerhouse Road
Potter Valley, CA 95469
743-1122
garlic, herbs, herb blends,
    sun-dried tomatoes, jams

MENDOCINO
BREWING COMPANY
P.O. Box 400
Hopland, CA 95449
744-1015
micro-brews

MENDOCINO BOUNTY
SPECIALTY MARKETPLACE
200 South School Street
Ukiah, CA 95482
463-6711
complete line of Mendocino-
    made preserves, condiments
    and wine

MENDOCINO
CHOCOLATE COMPANY
542 N. Main Street
Fort Bragg, CA 95437
964-8800
handmade truffles, chocolates,
    fudge sauce

MENDOCINO
JAMS & PRESERVES
Main Street
P.O. Box 781
Mendocino, CA 95460

retail and mail order jams,
    marmalades, dessert
    toppings, chutneys, mustard,
    ketchup and coffee

MENDOCINO
MINERAL WATER
Mendocino Beverages
1604 Fourth Street #2
Santa Rosa, CA 95404
522-2580
bottled mineral water

MENDOCINO
MUSHROOM COMPANY
18302 Georges Lane
Fort Bragg, CA 95437
964-1646
wild and exotic mushrooms

MENDOCINO
MUSHROOM FARM
31300 Chestnut Street
Fort Bragg, CA 95437
964-1935
wholesale cultivated
    mushrooms

MENDOCINO MUSTARD, INC.
1260 North Main Street
Fort Bragg, CA 95437
964-2250
original hot-sweet mustard;
    Seeds & Suds Mustard

MENDOCINO PASTA COMPANY
6819 Redwood Drive
Cotati, CA 94931
795-5859
dried, flavored premium pastas

MENDOCINO SEA VEGETABLES
P.O. Box 1265
Mendocino, CA 95460
937-2050
dried nori, wakame, sea palm
    frond, and more sea
    vegetables

MENDOCINO
SODA POP COMPANY
179 Jewett
Fort Bragg, CA 95437
964-4222
premium root beer

MOORE'S FLOUR MILL
1550 South State St.
Ukiah, CA 95437
462-6550
freshly milled flour, nuts,
    seeds, and many
    organic grains

MOUNTAIN FRESH
SPRING WATER COMPANY
P.O. Box 426
Fort Bragg, CA 95437
961-1138
bottled spring water

NORTH COAST
BREWING COMPANY
444 North Main Street
Fort Bragg, CA 95437
964-2739
premium micro-brewed beers

NOYO RESERVE LTD.
P.O. Box 2717
Fort Bragg, CA 95437
964-8142
mustards, salad dressings

OSCAR'S ENTERPRISES
P.O. Box 1404
Fort Bragg, CA 95437
964-1857
Sweet Basil, Romano salad
    dressings

P.J.'S GOURMET
1601 Deerwood Drive
Ukiah, CA 95482
462-1072
Stroh Ranch meat marinade

PAPA BEAR'S
CHOCOLATE HAUS
45150 Main Street
Mendocino, CA 95460
937-4406
taffy, chocolate covered
    nuts, caramels

PICKLES FROM THE SEA
39451 Comptche Road
Mendocino, CA 95460
937-5570
aged piquant vinegars,
    kelp pickles

QUESERIA MICHOACAN
9701 West Road
Redwood Valley, CA 95470
485-0638
cheese and ricotta

ROUND MAN'S SMOKE HOUSE
412 North Main Street
Fort Bragg, CA 95437
964-5954
retail and mail order: smoked
    sausages, pork, chicken, beef
    and salmon jerky, cheese,
    and more

ROYAL GARDENS TEAS
P.O. Box 1918
Fort Bragg, CA 95437
964-0118
premium teas

RUSSIAN RIVER
CEREAL COMPANY
4167 Eastside Calpella Road
Ukiah, CA 95482
485-8902
granola

RUSSIAN RIVER PISTACHIOS
P.O. Box 275
Calpella, CA 95418
462-3498
pistachios

SMITH RANCH
5301 Flynn Creek Road
Comptche, CA 95427
937-5745
ranch raised and fed beef,
    lamb, and pork

STORNETTA BROTHERS DAIRY
24450 South Highway 1
Point Arena, CA 95468
882-2531
wholesale milk and tours
    by appointment

STROH RANCH PRODUCE
14400 Eel River Road
Potter Valley, CA 95469
743-1463
vegetables, pies, cookies,
    cinnamon rolls

THANKSGIVING COFFEE
COMPANY
P.O. Box 1918
Fort Bragg, CA 95437
964-0118
premium coffees and teas

TOBINA'S SPECIALTY FOODS
P.O. Box 1467
Ukiah, CA 95482
468-8629
mustards, salad dressing,
    teriyaki sauce

TRES CLASSIQUE
P.O. Box 197
Redwood Valley, CA 95470
485-7749
salad dressings and sauces

TRILLIUM DELIGHTS
Northspur Station
Fort Bragg, CA 95437
459-5661
fruit conserves, dressing

INDEX

Allen, Ken, 74
Allen, Kimberly, 74
Allen, Tom, 75
Anderson Brewing Company, 74
Apple Farm, The, 78

Barkley, Don, 72
Barra Family, 56
Bates, Karen, 78
Bates, Tim, 78
Bennett, Ted, 48
Boonville, 74
Brandy Distillery
    Germain-Robin Alambic, Inc., 66
Brown-Forman, 28

Cafe Beaujolais Bakery and Brickery, 10, 82
Cahn, Deborah, 48
Caito Fisheries/Noyo Harbor, 86
Cheesecake Lady, The, 97
Cloverdale, 88
Coale, Ansley, 66
Collier, Robin, 97
Crawford, Bill, 44

Dudzik, Deny, 38

Eagle Rock Gourmet Lamb, 88

Fetzer Vinehards, 28
Fort Bragg, 75, 86, 98, 100
Fox, Margaret, 10, 82
Franks, Norman, 72
Frey Vineyards, 32
Frey, Jonathan, 32
Frey, Paul, 32

Germain-Robin, Hubert, 66
Gowan's Oak Tree Fruit Stand, 90
Gowan Family, 90
Green, Allan, 34
Greenwood Ridge Vineyards, 34

Handley Cellars, 38
Handley, Milla, 38
Hill, Bill, 54
Hopland, 28, 44, 72, 97
Husch Vineyards, 40

Jepson Vineyards, Winery, and Distillery, 42
Jepson, Alice, 42
Jepson, Robert, 42
Johnson, Stanley, 88

Katzeff, Joan, 100
Katzeff, Paul, 100
Keehn/Crawford Family, 44
Klein, Jim, 48
Kump, Christopher, 82

Laybourn, Michael, 72
Leviton, Paul, 97
Lorenzi, Kurt, 42
Louis Vuitton Moët Hennessey, 62
Lovett, Michael, 72

Martin, Dennis, 28
McDowell Valley Vineyards, 44
McFadden Farm, 94
McFadden, Guinness, 94
Meier, Fritz, 40
Mendocino Brewing Company, 72
Mendocino Specialty Retailers and Food
    Producers, 96

Navarro Vineyards, 48
North Coast Brewing Company, 75

Obester Winery, 52
Obester, Paul, 52
Obester, Sandy, 52
Oswald, H.A., Family, 40

Parducci Wine Cellars, 54
Pauli Family, 56
Philo, 34, 38, 40, 48, 52, 58, 62, 78, 90
Potter Valley, 94

Rasmussen, Stephen, 98
Record, Karen, 96
Redwood Valley Cellars, 56
Redwood Valley, 32, 56
Regalia, Bruce, 52
Roederer Estate, 58
Roederer, Louis, 58
Rosenthal, David, 56
Rosenthal, Joe, 75
Round Man's Smoke House, 98
Rouzaud, Jean-Claude, 58
Ruedrich, Mark, 75

Salgues, Michel, 58
Sawyer, Willis Tex, 62
Scahill, John, 72
Scharffenberger Cellars, 62
Scharffenberger, John, 62
Schmitt, Don, 78
Schmitt, Sally, 78

Thanksgiving Coffee Company, 100
Thomas Family, 102
Thorpe, Marilyn, 98
Towne, Dave, 74

Ukiah, 42, 54, 66, 96, 102